Frederick J Moss

Through Atolls and Islands in the Great South Sea

Frederick J Moss

Through Atolls and Islands in the Great South Sea

ISBN/EAN: 9783744730433

Printed in Europe, USA, Canada, Australia, Japan

Cover: Foto ©Andreas Hilbeck / pixelio.de

More available books at **www.hansebooks.com**

H

ATOLLS

ANDS

E

UTH SEA

J. MOSS

Presented to
The Library
of the
University of Toronto
by

D. F. Craigie, Esq.,
24 Glendonwynne Rd.,
Toronto 9, Ont.

THROUGH ATOLLS

AND ISLANDS IN THE GREAT SOUTH SEA

BY

FREDERICK J. MOSS, M.H.R.

(MEMBER OF THE HOUSE OF REPRESENTATIVES, NEW ZEALAND)

LONDON
SAMPSON LOW, MARSTON, SEARLE, & RIVINGTON
Limited
St. Dunstan's House
FETTER LANE, FLEET STREET, E.C.
1889

PREFACE.

The "Great South Sea" has been a region of romance from the day when De Balboa in the year of grace, 1513, so named the new ocean which burst upon his view as he gazed to the south from the hills above Panama. The exploits of buccaneers, the work of explorers and missionaries, the strange customs and the grace kindliness and ferocity of the islanders, have been the theme of many a well-known writer. The old order is changing and the more sober era of commerce rapidly rising in its place. Having had opportunities of observing both epochs, I wish to portray, as simply and faithfully as I can, the men and the customs of each. In doing so, it may be impossible to avoid running counter to cherished opinions, and still more cherished interests, but I have set down nothing without careful inquiry or the best assurance of substantial truth which the circumstances would permit.

My notes were made more than two years ago, during a seven months' voyage among the least frequented groups. A few changes have since occurred, but I have thought it better to treat them separately, and to give the story as written at the time.

AUCKLAND, NEW ZEALAND.
August, 1889.

CONTENTS.

CHAPTER I.

THE VOYAGE AND HOW IT CAME ABOUT.

PAGE

Fiji in 1868—Defeat of the *Challenger's* boats—New Zealand settlers in Fiji—The present discontent—Cruise of the *Buster*—Arrival at Niuè—Rev. Frank Lawes—Churches at Niuè—Commodore Goodenough—Native liquor laws—Disease and its ravages—Niuè to Christmas Island—Suwarrow—England's "latest colony"—Wreck of the *Diana*—Shipwrecked mariners—Rescued from Starbuck—Swain's Island—Copra and its profits—Mr. Eli Jennings—Through the Archipelagoes   1

CHAPTER II.

ATOLLS AND ISLANDS.

Formation of coral reefs—Atolls or lagoon islands—The Milli atoll—Coral gardens—The lagoon islanders—Food and dress—The water difficulty—The old navigators—Jaluit, the German metropolis—The embryo city—A small paradise—Jaluit lagoon—Lagoon island products—The work of the polyp—Pearls and pearl oysters—

Spaniards and the pearl islands—Beauties and drawbacks—Landing at a lagoon island—Bird islands—Raised coral islands — Mountainous islands—The home of the cocoanut—Hamburg merchants—English influence 26

CHAPTER III.

PAST AND PRESENT.

Spain's lost position—The old buccaneers—First missionary ship—French acquisitions—The whaling era—The kidnapping period—Peruvian kidnappers—English kidnappers—The sandal-wood era—Bêche de Mer—Pearl divers—Cocoanut oil and copra—Rich tropical products—Missionaries, traders, and natives—The innocent savage—The fate of Benjamin Boyd—Some innocent murders—A marvellous monarch—Dr. Dana at Fakaafu—Changed habits—Eccentric hats . . . 53

CHAPTER IV.

SOME OLD-FASHIONED CELEBRITIES.

The trader of the old school—The trader of to-day—In the Majuro Lagoon—Bully Hayes—Hayes at Manihiki—His doings at Ujilan—To windward of his pursuers—Steals the *Lotus* at San Francisco—His exploits in the *Pioneer*—Renames her the *Leonore*—Future Hayes impossible—Modern communications—Modern trading establishments—Samoa, Tonga, and Germany 80

CHAPTER V.

A FEW PACIFIC ISLANDERS.

Passengers in the *Buster*—An "Ocean" Islander—The Eastern Islanders—Tongans, Tahitians, and Samoans—Origin of the races—Island characteristics—George Ellis of Manihiki—His early experiences—His account of Penrhyn—Description of Manihiki—King Apollo—Manihiki Turimen—Queer laws and customs—Old Rupè and the ghost woman—Maories and witches—Religious observance—A contrast in native missionaries—The curfew at Manihiki—The *Gente Hermosa*—Missionary responsibilities 97

CHAPTER VI.

SOME KINGS AND OTHER PEOPLE.

George Ellis gives his opinions—King Jibberik of Majuro—Jibberik's wars and conquests—Leilikè defies the Booloo-man—Jibberik's newest ambition—Leilikè's sad fate—A few other kings—Caste among the natives—King Tembainookè—His dominions and practices—His harem—Laziness unsurpassed and unsurpassable—Pleasant Island—Pleasant Islanders at deadly feud—A tour at Pleasant Island—How they fortify their houses—How they shoot each other—Europeans safe if out of the line of fire—Origin of the strife—Easily disarmed—Introduction of the "Hellish" toddy—An old Pleasant Island trader . . 120

CHAPTER VII.

MISSIONARY WORK IN THE PACIFIC.

Rigid observances—Missionaries and the Areois—Results of the conflict—Meaning of conversion—A transition state—Absence of amusement—Want of mental occupation—Mischievous prohibitions—The Turi and its ways at Manihiki—The stocks—Feud of missionary and trader—Connubial relations—Teaching English—The Rev. Robert Logan—His station at Ruk—Missionary labours at Lukunor—Weaving at Lukunor—Churches in the Western Pacific—Churches in the East—Roman Catholic Church—Respective spheres of operation—Characteristic difficulties—Hard laws and a trader's opinion—Necessity for healthy pastimes—A new departure imperative . 147

CHAPTER VIII.

A VISIT TO PONAPÈ, ITS RUINS, AND ITS PEOPLE.

The products of Ponapè—On the road to China and Japan—Pagans and Christians—Ravages of small-pox—At Kusaie by the way—At Pingelap and Mokal—Pet dogs—Pet Frigate birds—Spanish man-of-war—Mr. Kubarri's work—Start for the ruins—A trader's hospitality—The islets on the reef—Massive and mysterious ruins—Who were the builders?—Native migrations—A pleasure trip from Atafu—Islanders born rovers—Islets of Ponapè apparently coral—A rough passage—Native customs—Heathen and Christian at

Kite—Mr. Begg of Ponapè—His career and opinions—Captain Edward Rodd, a Pacific celebrity—His early experiences and present opinions—Good-bye to the veterans—Recent slaughter of Spanish governor and forty-five soldiers at Ponapè 177

CHAPTER IX.

A CROWN COLONY OF A SEVERE TYPE.

Old Fiji—"A land of tyrants and a den of slaves"—Cakobau as a boy—His conflicts with missionaries—Commodore Wilkes at Fiji—Fijian savagery—Cakobau in 1868—The American claims—The Polynesian company—Fiji in 1869—Fijians and planters—Beginnings of Government—The Fijian Crown of 1867—Government in 1869—Government finally formed (1871)—King and constitution—Meeting of Parliament (1871)—Conflict in constitution—Resignation of ministers—The Wood-Thurston Ministry—They dispense with Parliament—British subjects' Mutual Protection Society—Crown colony in 1874—Sir Arthur Gordon as governor—Degradation of the Union Jack—The blessed rule of the Colonial Office—Laying foundation for future ills—Justice to the weak 215

CHAPTER X.

ENGLAND AND OTHER POWERS.

The "mutual" declaration—Germany's sphere—England's sphere—Unsatisfactory omissions—French missionaries—Spain as a Pacific power—French convict settlement—Origin of German claims—Johan Cæsar Godeffroi and Co.—Their rise and fall—"Die Deutsche Handels- und Plantagen-Gesellschaft zum Süd See Inseln," commonly known as the Long Handle Co.—The iron money—The "See-Handels-Gesellschaft"—Prince Bismarck's guarantee—Failure to float new company—Our diplomatists—The High Commissioner—The High Court—Arbitrary powers——Judge Gorrie in evidence—Bias of the High Court—Foreign men-of-war—Cases in point—A Deputy High Commissioner—Her Majesty's ships—The Hawaiian kingdom—Tonga and her troubles—The Rev. Shirley Baker—King George of Tonga—The new National Church of Tonga—German annexation of Samoa—King Mahetou of Samoa—Braver and better counsels . . . 248

APPENDIX A.

Showing how land titles were registered in Fiji in 1862 283

APPENDIX B.

Private Circular sent to the Planters preliminary to an attempted formation of Native Government in 1870 286

APPENDIX C.

Government Gazette of June 10, 1871, containing official notification of the constitution of a Government under King Cakobau . . 295

APPENDIX D.

Proclamation of June 9, 1871, reviving the lapsed constitution of 1867, and convening a meeting of Delegates for August 1, 1871 . . . 298

APPENDIX E.

Oath of allegiance to Cakobau by 297 chiefs in 1867 . 300

APPENDIX F.

King Cakobau's address at the opening of the first Parliament, Nov. 3, 1871 . . . 302

APPENDIX G.

Secret circular inviting to the formation of a British Subjects' Mutual Protection Society " to overturn a usurping ministry by armed force, if necessary" (Jan. 20th, 1873) . . . 306

APPENDIX H.

Convention between Great Britain and Germany as to spheres of respective influence in the Western Pacific (April 6, 1886) . . . 310

APPENDIX I.

Steam lines now at work between Europe and the various colonies and settlements in the Pacific . 315

LIST OF ILLUSTRATIONS.

Portrait of Author .	*Frontispiece.*	
Mission Residence, Niuè . . .	*To face page*	9
Interior large native Church at Alofi, Niuè	,,	11
Interior of Church, Lukunor ⋅ roughly built of hewn timber, but elaborately ornamented	,,	25
At Manihiki, showing part of the reef on the ocean face of the Islet and Lagoon, with other islets in the background .	,,	29
Coast scene, Niuè, Savage Island . .	,,	46
Cocoanut Palm in full bearing, Swain's Island	,,	68
Group at Atafu Lagoon (showing also women's fashionable "paper" hats)	,,	78
Trader's house (George Ellis), Manihiki	,,	104
King Aporo's house, Manihiki . . .	,,	109
Group at Majuro, Lagoon (Marshall Islands): boys, girls, and women in front of native house . . .	,,	123
King Jibberik of Majuro	,,	127
Pleasant Island Warrior .	,,	136
Native Church, Manihiki . . .	,,	168
Exterior view of Church at Mokal in grove of bread-fruit trees	,,	184
Girl of Mokal, Caroline Islands .	,,	186
View of Jamestown Harbour, Ponapè	,,	188
Front view of great ruins at Ponapè .	,,	193
Ground-plan of ruins at Ponapè	,,	194

THROUGH ATOLLS AND ISLANDS

IN THE

GREAT SOUTH SEA.

CHAPTER I.

THE VOYAGE AND HOW IT CAME ABOUT.

Fiji in 1868—Defeat of the *Challenger's* boats—New Zealand settlers in Fiji—The present discontent—Cruise of the *Buster*—Arrival at Niuè—Rev. Frank Lawes—Churches at Niuè—Commodore Goodenough—Native liquor laws—Disease and its ravages—Niuè to Christmas Island—Suwarrow—England's "latest colony"—Wreck of the *Diana*—Shipwrecked mariners—Rescued from Starbuck—Swain's Island—Copra and its profits—Mr. Eli Jennings—Through the Archipelagos.

NEARLY thirty years ago I stood on the beach of the then little seaport of Lyttelton watching with keen interest the departure of a small cutter for the distant islands of Fiji. Chartered by Mr. Reece, a prosperous ironmonger in the neighbouring nine-year-old city of Christchurch, the little craft was bent on a prospecting voyage to the mystic islands which many of us longed to see. The voyage, full of risk, was prompted by the same adventurous spirit that had given New Zealand itself to the empire and played so large a part in spreading the flag and the commerce of England over the habitable globe.

Mr. Reece brought back a glowing account of the Fiji Islands. Later on, when the American civil war made sea-island cotton precious in the markets of the world, several New Zealanders, myself among the number, determined to try what could be done in cotton-growing in Fiji. The owner of a small trading schooner, the *Banshee*, was induced to fit up her hold for our accommodation and we availed ourselves of the rare chance of making the trip to and from those islands, then almost isolated from the rest of the world.

On our arrival we found that the coast tribes had been converted to Christianity. At all events they had abandoned cannibalism and cut short their enormous bushy heads of hair, very rigidly observed the Sabbath and daily flocked, at the beat of the *Lali*, to morning and evening prayer.

Of all this we had seen a good deal among the Maoris of our own colony and were not perhaps so deeply impressed as we otherwise should have been.

The mountain tribes were still heathen and cannibal. Only a year before they had killed and eaten the Rev. Mr. Baker, a Wesleyan missionary who insisted on passing through their country in spite of the repeated warnings of the chief. The hereditary enemy of the mountaineers was Cakobau, paramount chief of the coast tribes and the mainstay of the missionaries. In their own rude way the mountaineers connected Mr. Baker with their powerful enemy and feared that his mission foreboded their subjection. Mr. Baker's persistence in advancing gave intensity to the fear and led to the sad ending of his exploration. This was the account given to us at the time and subsequently confirmed by personal intercourse with the mountaineers.

Soon after we arrived, these same mountaineers successfully drove back the armed boats of H.M.S. *Challenger* when attempting to penetrate, by the River Rewa, to a place called Diuka in the same hills which had proved so fatal to poor Baker. The result of this disaster was the forced abandonment of the few plantations begun on the Upper Rewa. The planters were loth to go, asked for arms and offered to hold their own against the enemy. Commodore Lambert refused the arms but kindly offered them a passage in the *Challenger*, to be landed destitute and penniless in Sydney. They of course declined the offer. The affair was frightfully mismanaged. The Commodore had given orders that the sailors were on no account to be landed, otherwise the Fijians would have been assuredly driven back and taught a lesson of permanent value.

The white population of Fiji was not above 400 souls, scattered on plantations over all parts of the group or engaged in business in the little township of Levuka. The natives numbered 140,000. There was no government, but there were also no taxes nor impediments of any kind to prevent a man entering on whatever calling or business he might prefer. Careful observation satisfied most of our party that we might safely settle in the country; that the few settlers already there were people with whom we might be glad to live; that the natives were not likely to molest us and were too much divided by tribal feuds to be permanently dangerous if they did.

We numbered twenty-three men in all, crowded in the hold of the little *Banshee*. Several bought land in different parts of the country and began work at once. Others also bought land and arranged with the natives to build houses while they returned to New Zealand for their families. In my own case the contract made with a chief of the Rewa district was unusually large. The house was to be forty feet square with a verandah all round, and to be put up within three months. The walls, roof, and verandah were to be built for the sum of thirty dollars (£6) with a bonus of three dollars on satisfactory completion. It was built of reeds tied together with vines and native-made cord. Not a nail was used, but the house proved convenient and comfortable till blown over three years later.

Returning from New Zealand with my family to Fiji, the first crop of cotton was put in and gathered within a year. My plantation was on the Upper Rewa and large numbers of natives of different tribes came to work, as many occasionally as 200 at one time. Among them were many of the dreaded mountaineers who proved quiet, bright, and cheerful workers. The good relations thus established with them were not disturbed during my residence in Fiji.

In those early days the life and travelling were necessarily rough, but settlers from New Zealand and Australia poured in quickly and we were soon nearly 2000 strong. The influx was one of educated, earnest settlers who bought their land fairly and openly from the Fijians, registered their titles in the British Consulate, and set to work promptly on their isolated plantations.

Such was Fiji in 1868 when settlement first set in strongly from New Zealand and Australia. Ill-health drove me to Auckland, for we had no doctors in Fiji. To my great regret, further residence in the tropics was forbidden, but the prohibition proved a blessing in disguise. It saved me from the fate of many of my old compeers whom I met again only last year in Fiji. They had gone there with sanguine hopes and fair prospect of success, but after spending their capital and giving to the work the best years of their life were now heart-crushed and hopeless. Can it be surprising that they were also filled with a bitter hatred towards the Government and the Colonial Office by whom they had been practically enslaved, and to whose perverse blundering the destruction of their fair prospects was largely due? Immigration to Fiji had long ceased. All had left who could and no settler now thinks of making a home in that beautiful and fertile group. Nor is any likely to do so while the present un-English and degrading system of government is suffered to exist.

In New Zealand and in Fiji I had gained some knowledge of the Southern and Central Pacific, but the islands and myriad islets of the outer lagoon world were a sealed book still. They are not easily visited, the only communication being by casual trading-vessels each with its own distinct line of traffic. Gladly availing myself of an offer from the well-known Auckland firm of Henderson and Macfarlane, I took passage in the schooner *Buster* which they were sending to make, for the first time, a complete round of their old stations and to find proper sites for establishing new. There was the further advantage that in a trading-vessel the natives would be seen as they are, and not as they get themselves up for the passing visit of a man-of-war, a High Commissioner, or an inspecting Missionary.

The *Buster* was commanded by Captain

Theet, a skilful and vigilant sailor, a Schleswig Dane who had left his country to avoid being made a German. My fellow-passengers were the supercargo, Mr. Geo. Dunnett, and an Auckland photographer, Mr. Andrew. The former was experienced in the island trade and in the ways of the natives and to his help I am indebted for access to sources of information not otherwise so readily obtained. Mr. Andrew made a splendid collection of photographs during the voyage and to him I am also indebted for the illustrations which he kindly gave me leave to select from his unique collection.

We left Auckland on the 18th of September, 1886, and after a passage of eighteen days made our first point, Niuè, about 1000 miles west of Tahiti. Niuè is the "Savage Island" of Cook, and was named by him from a peculiarity of the natives who, when excited or angry, still rush about with eyes gleaming and beards held between the teeth. For all that, they are a pleasant enough people, fond of migrating to other islands for work and regarded as excellent labourers on colonial plantations.

Niuè is a coral island, between forty and

Mission Residence at Alofi, Niué.

fifty miles in circumference, and rising to a height of 200 feet. The population is returned in the missionary census as 5070 resident, with 503 absentees all married men, and temporarily at other islands. About one-half of the population consists of adult men and women, the other half of children. The decomposed coral soil is shallow but very productive, and Niuè yams are renowned for their quality. The fruits and coffee, the cotton, sugar-cane and arrowroot are all of the best description, while the climate is cool, dry, and admirable.

We spent three pleasant days at Niuè, the most pleasant of the voyage. The island has the advantage of a resident missionary and his family and the effect is apparent in the manners and habits of the people. If all missionaries were like the Rev. Frank Lawes of Niuè, large-minded, sympathetic and educated men, the native teachers who are trained and sent forth to smaller islands would be very different to many of whose strange pranks I shall have to speak by-and-by. Aided by his wife, a lady as devoted to the work as himself, Mr. Lawes finds constant employment in training and teaching the natives and in travelling over his rough, roadless island. He is also completing a new translation of the Scriptures into the Niuè tongue which is distinct from that of the adjacent islands.

The natives have built very fine churches at Alofi and Avatele, two villages a couple of miles apart and situated at the end of the island where the most convenient landing-places are to be found.

The Niuè people still follow many of their old customs, the way of burying the dead being one of the most curious. Each defunct is buried on his or her own land, and as this is never extensive the tomb is close to the house of the deceased. The roadways are lined on each side with these tombs. If the dead man has been a sailor, the plastered coral mound over the grave takes the form of a ship, with perhaps a grotesque imitation of a sailor for the figure-head. The variety in tombs is considerable, and very often some of the articles in personal use by the deceased are placed upon them. On one a teacup and saucer may be seen, on another an earthenware dish or plate or similar relics which remain religiously untouched till they break or decay. These tombs are conspicuous objects along every road in Niuè.

Interior of large Native Church at Alofi, Niué.

Copyright. Photographed by Mr. Andrew.

The interior of the church at Alofi is particularly striking. The structure is of coral stone, large and well built, ninety feet in length and twenty-five feet in width. At Avatele the church is larger and much more elaborately finished, but the interior effect is not equal to that produced by the long vista of simple, massive and sloping tree trunks which support the lofty roof of the church at Alofi.

Hard and unceasing is the work of a zealous missionary in an island like Niuè. He is not only the teacher but the adviser and confidant of every native chief, the one to whom the native naturally turns in time of public trouble or domestic difficulty. Great is the missionary's relief when the natives can be induced to unite for the common good. Throughout the islands native councils have thus been formed, very curious in their operation and in the laws which they make. At Niuè several attempts have been made in this direction but with only partial success. Sir Arthur Gordon, when Governor of Fiji and High Commissioner, paid a visit to the island and tried to induce the natives to add themselves to his dominions. They had heard, however, of the vain regrets of the people of Rotumah who had been persuaded into taking this course, and they respectfully declined a remedy worse than the disease.

The lamented Commodore Goodenough called once at Niuè, just as a meeting was being held to consider the formation of a suitable government. He addressed the natives at their own request. Some wished to set up a king but the Commodore advised them first to settle, with some degree of unanimity, who the king should be. They appreciated this advice and came to the conclusion that it would be better to have no king at all for the present. Since then the Niuè people have established a council of representatives elected every two months by the heads of families, and the nucleus perhaps of something bigger if not better hereafter. The native dwellings are verandahed cottages, built of wattle and well plastered with locally burned lime. Peeping out from groves of cocoanut and orange trees, these pretty white cottages make an attractive picture and show that the people are an improvable race. Tall palms tower above the little houses and the date-palm grows well in Mr. Lawes' own garden. The fruit is abundant but falls off before ripening, from what cause has not yet been ascertained.

The rigid prohibition of intoxicating liquor is a favourable feature at Niuè, as in all the missionary islands. There is nothing in the life, habits, or tastes of the natives to make the use of intoxicants in the least degree necessary, and their circumstances render exclusion easy. Unfortunately, exclusion is not so easy with disease of the most virulent kind which is doing terrible mischief throughout the islands and causing deep anxiety to all who care for the welfare of the people. England or Australasia could do nothing more beneficent to these islanders than despatch a proper commission to report upon the subject and to devise, if possible, a suitable remedy. We hear much about the traffic in firearms and drink, but both are trifles in comparison with the ravages of a disease terrible to the living and threatening extermination to these poor, kindly, isolated people. Men, women, and children suffer alike, and no traveller can look upon their wasted forms without commiseration. Why should this continue? Christianity and humanity call aloud for energetic and immediate action. The subject is not one with which missionary reports can deal in sufficient fulness to impress the public mind, but to every missionary the facts are well known and excite profound anxiety.

As the reader becomes better acquainted with the conditions under which the natives live in these distant islands, with the absence of medical skill and the entire dependence on some trader or native missionary teacher as doctor, he will better understand the gravity of the question. Would that my voice were strong enough to call to it the notice it deserves, to bring home to benevolent minds the present suffering and ultimate extinction which the fell disease, if left unchecked, must entail on these bright and helpless people.

Niuè was a good preparation for the subsequent voyage. We there witnessed the beneficent effect which a large and true piety, accompanied by taste and refinement, must exercise on all who are brought within its influence. Henceforth we were to travel from island to island over many thousand miles of ocean in which the place of the European missionary is filled by a native teacher. And such teachers! There are exceptions, of course, but as a rule they are ignorant, pompous, greedy and narrow-minded, either untrainable or trained under influences sadly differing from those which have done so much to advance the people of the beautiful little coral island of Niuè.

We resumed our voyage on the evening of the 9th of October, steered north and east, called at Manihiki, Suwarrow, and other islands, and reached Christmas Island lying three degrees north of the line. This island is also one of Cook's discoveries. He sighted it on Christmas Day, 1777, and remained till January 2nd of the following year observing an eclipse and catching turtle, of which he tells us he succeeded in getting 300 weighing from ninety to 100 pounds each. I reserve for future chapters a description of this and of the numerous other islands at which we called; but may mention that Christmas is perhaps the largest lagoon island in the Pacific. In circuit it exceeds 100 miles. The great lagoon in the centre is comparatively shallow and abounds in pearl shell. The island was treeless and uninhabited when taken up some years ago by Messrs. Henderson and Macfarlane. They have planted many thousand cocoanuts, developed the pearl fishery, and will no doubt make the island in course of time a valuable property.

Since my visit to Christmas, the flag is said to have been hoisted and the island made part of the British dominions. The entrance to the lagoon is poor and adapted only for boats and small craft; but there is excellent anchorage under the lee side of the island. Suwarrow, at which we also called, is an atoll of very different character and of which the same Auckland firm has been for some years in possession. There too they have planted on a considerable scale, built stores and a wharf and established a pearl fishery. But the Suwarrow lagoon is easy of access to the largest ocean steamers, affords splendid anchorage and lies on the direct route between Panama and New Zealand. French men-of-war from Tahiti know it well. By English or other vessels-of-war it is never visited; but the sooner Suwarrow is placed under the British flag the better. The lagoon must become of considerable importance when an Inter-Oceanic Canal is opened, apart from its value as a centre for trading with the many surrounding islands. Let us hope that no blundering convention will be made with France similar to that already made with Germany, and that we shall not wake up one morning to find

Suwarrow, like Rapa, included in the French possessions.

Among the islands which we passed on our way to Christmas, was Starbuck Island, "England's latest Colony in the Pacific" as it was styled by a leading London journal in an article which we colonists should call a splendid "blow" on the opening of the Indian and Colonial Exhibition. Good heavens, what a colony! A low, bare, coral rock four miles long and less than a couple of miles wide, without a single tree, semblance of harbour or decent landing-place. Starbuck is a worked-out, deserted guano islet, to which vessels of all kinds carefully give the widest berth and at which we only called to rescue four mariners whom we heard were shipwrecked on its surf-bound shore.

It came about in this wise. At Manihiki we found the captain of the Swedish Bark *Diana* and seven of her crew, who told us they had been wrecked at Starbuck three months before when carrying a cargo of timber from Puget Sound to Sydney. They landed safely at Starbuck and remained for two months hoping relief. None came, so they decided to take the only boat they had saved and seek help at Maldon Island, another barren guano islet not yet exhausted and about 150 miles from Starbuck. Only eight of the party could be taken in the boat and lots were drawn to settle who should be left behind. The boat started with fair weather but wind failed and the current was against them. They were obliged to give up their original intention and make for Manihiki which they reached in nineteen days, after a voyage in their crowded boat of more than 600 miles.

They approached Manihiki with dread believing that the natives were still what the Swedish captain called " wild mans ;" but great was their delight at seeing on the shore a crowd dressed in European clothing. Running the boat through the surf, they landed and were received with the warm hospitality for which the people of Manihiki are renowned. The shipwrecked men had only been a few days at Manihiki when we arrived and they were much disappointed at finding that our course carried us farther afield, so that they must wait another opportunity to get away. But the men were comfortable and well cared for and our captain promised that he would, if possible, call at Starbuck and take off the comrades they had been obliged to leave on that barren isle.

A fortnight later we made Starbuck at two in the afternoon. Fortunately the day was fine and a strong breeze enabled us to close in with the shore and sail along in search of a suitable spot for a boat to pass through the breakers. The *Diana* was lying on the reef, a complete wreck with her cargo of timber being gradually smashed to pieces in the surf. The men had hung a large tablecloth to a pole and we observed then running to and fro as we approached. It was impossible to get close enough to communicate from the ship and a boat was sent to what appeared a practicable point.

After pulling for some distance along the edge of the reef the boat was obliged to return as night closed in. The current being very strong we were forced to put to sea again and leave the poor fellows, whom we could see slowly and with downcast heads walking back to the hut they had built for shelter.

During the night the wind increased almost to a gale but the captain was determined not to abandon the rescue without further effort. Next morning Starbuck was out of sight. Fortunately we made it again during the forenoon, and the boat managed to effect a landing on the end of the island opposite to that along which we had coasted the day before. The shipwrecked men were not to be seen but we observed two of our boatmen running across the ocky island. They went to help the men fearing that they might be too ill or weak to face the four miles of rough stony land between them and the boat. Time passed and as night came on the anxiety was great lest we should be blown out to sea and our own men with the others be left behind.

Anxiously we watched the place, but there lay the boat drawn up on the beach with two of the men left in charge and no sign of movement on the shore. Just at sunset two men could be seen slowly making their way to the boat, but darkness set in with tropical suddenness. We were obliged to stand off and on with the ship and our boatmen made a fire ashore so that we could keep the spot in view. What intense relief when out of the darkness we heard the distant "Coo-ee" of Bill the steersman, a Rotumah man to whose skilful care the boat had been committed. How gladly we welcomed them on board! It was a weight from all our minds, but more especially from that of Captain Theet whose noble perseverance saved these men from a prolonged and dreary residence, perhaps from death, on the bare and barren shore of our "Latest Colony."

We afterwards learned, what is worth noting for the possible benefit of others, that a small opening blown out of the reef by the Guano Company, offers a boat passage for landing in fair weather. It was in the neighbourhood of this passage that the men had gathered the day before, expecting the boat to land there. Next day when the vessel was again sighted, the poor fellows were in doubt as to where the boat would land and had scattered over the island to be on the look-out. Hence the delay in their getting together afterwards. The boat opening, it may be as well to state, is just opposite the ruins of the Company's old buildings at the N.W. point of the island. We also learned later on that the trading schooner *Malolo*, from Honolulu, promised to call at the island as it was not known for some months that we had succeeded in getting the men on board. The *Malolo* made several attempts but was baulked by the current and failed in getting to the island at all. The greater, therefore, the credit due to Captain Theet for the rescue, and it seems to me that if ever man deserved the medal of a Humane Society, or recognition from the Government of Sweden, he earned it on this occasion. The consciousness of a good deed has, so far, been the only and I doubt not to him sufficient reward.[1]

From Christmas Island we again turned south and called at Swain's Island, a small coral gem not three miles long and about one mile broad. Swain's is a little distant from the Union group and was taken up about twenty-five years ago by Mr. Eli Jennings, an American, who settled upon the islet with his wife the daughter of a Samoan chief. He planted cocoa-nuts and made as much oil as want of capital and the cumbrous processes of the period allowed. By-and-by the system of drying the nut for exportation was introduced into the islands by the German firm of Godeffroi and Co. The great difficulty of getting casks and the extra labour in making and handling the oil were thus avoided. Mr. Jennings increased his plantations and worked with new energy till his death about ten years ago. His sons followed in his footsteps

---

[1] Captain Theet, I am glad to say, has since received from the Swedish Government a handsome gold medal in recognition of his services on this occasion.

and last year exported 210 tons copra valued, on the spot, at 10*l.* per ton. In three to five years the whole of the plantations on their little islet will be in full bearing and they look for a steady increase up to 600 tons. Six thousand pounds a year from so small an islet, and obtained with so little labour and expense that, beyond a dozen Tanna men, the whole work is done by the family now numbering nearly fifty souls from the infant in arms to the aged widow of the founder of the enterprise.

The little islet can scarcely contain 2000 acres in the whole. The centre is occupied by a very beautiful salt-water lagoon which (with the sea beaches) must take up half the area. On the remainder, surrounding the lagoon, the plantations of cocoanut for copra, and of food for home use, have been made. The cocoanut is slow-growing but wonderfully productive and long-lived, yielding perhaps the largest return with the smallest risk and least cost of any plant in the world. These coral islands are its natural home. The nut is placed in a shallow cavity scooped out of the thin coral soil, an iron nail or bit of iron hoop run into the husk to accelerate the growth, and the cultivator has little more to do than wait patiently some ten or twelve years for his return.

There are no weeds to be kept down as in richer soils, and there is little expense in thinning and replanting as failures in growth are comparatively rare. Our stay at Swain's Island was only for the day. There is no anchorage and the *Buster* had as usual to stand off and on while we landed through the surf and hauled the boat up on the steep little beach of coral sand.

The day was very pleasantly passed. Mr. Jennings has made numerous roads through his little domain, has imported light carts to carry the nuts to the copra shed, and two light buggies from San Francisco in which he drove us round the island. The families are Samoan and preserve many of their Samoan tastes and habits, but his own house is filled with handsome furniture and abounds in works of art and other unexpected luxuries. He has also built a very pretty little church and the native missionary teaches the numerous children by whom he is surrounded. We saw all that was to be seen and shall long retain pleasant memories of his hospitable place, so rich in its returns, so lovely, and yet so isolated that he has to depend on the casual trading-vessels which call three or four times a year, for an opportunity of going to Samoa when he desires to do so.

Interior of Church, Lukunor.

Through the islands of the adjacent Union (Tokerau) group, through the Ellice, the Gilbert (Kingsmill), and the Marshall Archipelagos we wended our way, finishing with the Carolines into which we penetrated some 1200 miles. Numerous were the detached islands at which the *Buster* also called. At last we reached Lukunor, one of the loveliest of lagoon islands and only about 800 miles from Yap the most westerly of the Carolines. Germany has trading and coaling stations at Yap, which island was the cause of the recent hot dispute between that country and Spain.

At Lukunor we spent a week refitting and thence sailed straight for Auckland, where we arrived after a passage of forty-six days and an absence of seven months. We had crossed the Equator six times, visited more than forty islands, and returned to hear of deaths and changes, of Russian, and German, and French wars narrowly averted, of Irish excitements, and of events that had stirred the great world but of which not the faintest echo had reached us during the voyage. What I saw and whom I met during these seven months and the conclusions suggested by the experience, will be found in the chapters that follow.

CHAPTER II.

ATOLLS AND ISLANDS.

Formation of coral reefs—Atolls or lagoon islands—The Milli atoll—Coral gardens—The lagoon islanders—Food and dress—The water difficulty—The old navigators—Jaluit, the German metropolis—The embryo city—A small paradise—Jaluit lagoon—Lagoon island products—The work of the polyp—Pearls and pearl oysters—Spaniards and the pearl islands—Beauties and drawbacks—Landing at a lagoon island—Bird islands—Raised coral islands—Mountainous islands—The home of the cocoanut—Hamburg merchants—English influence.

THE islands and archipelagos scattered over so vast an area and so bewildering in name and number, are susceptible of easy classification. Three well-marked types prevail, namely, the atoll or lagoon island, the raised coral island, and the high mountainous island. Take, through the tropical part of the ocean, a diagonal line beginning in the south and east at the Paumotus and ending in the north and west at the far Pelews. On the northern side of this line innumerable atolls will be found but islands of other kinds be rarely seen. On the southern side the conditions are reversed, raised coral islands or high mountainous islands abound while the atoll is the rare exception.

Modern geology disputes the Darwinian theory of coral formation. For our present purpose that theory may be still accepted and the diagonal line regarded as dividing an area of gradual subsidence on the northern side from an area of equally gradual elevation on the southern. During long ages, as the land was imperceptibly sinking, the reef-building Polyp raised its great bastion on the mountain flanks and kept pace with the slowly submerging mass. The combined movement ended in the formation of the great reef, an eternal monument of the mountains buried beneath the waters of the lagoon which it encloses. On the tops of the mountains, as they sank beneath the lagoon, the coral continued to build, forming the rock patches of greater or less extent characteristic of them all.

Darwin, Dana, and other eminent men have eloquently expounded this theory of the formation of atolls, and raised coral islands. The latter were held to be only the atoll with a shallow lagoon gradually filled with coral *débris*, and the whole elevated by submarine forces until a solid island, never exceeding 100 to 200 feet at its highest point, was the result. These theories were based on the belief that the reef-building Polyp cannot exist at a greater depth than 120 feet, can flourish only in water of the greatest clearness and purity, and must have a solid rock foundation for its infant home. A new theory has been developed by the researches of Mr. John Murray, Naturalist of H.M.S. *Challenger*, and strengthened by subsequent discoveries in the Solomon Islands made by Dr. Guppy, Surgeon of H.M. surveying vessel *Lark*. The new theory is held to meet the ascertained facts more naturally and more completely, but the Darwinian view still enables us to form a clear conception of those wonderful works, built during countless ages with the skeletons of inconceivable myriads of the little Polyp.

The Paumotus (Cloud of Islands), at which our imaginary line began, are remarkable for the richness of their pearls and pearl shell, and the wild, daring character of their people. They are situated in the Eastern Pacific near the world-famed Tahiti. The Pelews, at the other

Manihiki.

Copyright. Photographed by Mr. Andrew.

end of the line, were famous in their day as the country of the amiable Prince Lee Boo, whose visit and untimely death created a sensation in London nearly a century ago. They lie in the Western Pacific 5000 miles from the Paumotus, and over the intervening expanse of water the atoll world is spread. Through a great part of this world the voyage of the *Buster* was made.

The name Atoll is of Maldive origin. The potentate who rules over that group styles himself "Sultan of the Thirteen Atollons and Twelve Thousand Isles." In one sense the title is only a mild Oriental exaggeration, each Atollon consisting of a salt-water lagoon and a number of islets—sometimes a very large number—strung together at irregular intervals on the narrow surface of the surrounding coral reef. The islet-covered reef hems in the deep lagoon which it has cut off from the surrounding ocean. Its characteristic features are the steepness and great depth of the reef-walls, and the narrowness, flatness, and low level of the islets formed upon its surface. Few lagoons are less than ten miles long, and three or four miles broad. The majority are much larger, some being of great size. The lagoon of Naira, in the Paumotus is described by Dr. Dana as fifty miles long and twenty broad. The *Buster* did not call at Naira, but did so at Milli (in the Marshall Archipelago), which will be a good illustration of one of these larger lagoons.

The Milli atoll, about thirty miles long and twelve to fifteen broad, cannot be seen from a ship's deck in the clearest weather at a greater distance than ten to twelve miles. Even then it is only the tops of the tall cocoanut-trees on the islets that are visible. The land is about twelve feet above the sea, as a rule, but in some parts a few feet higher. Approaching Milli, the long line of breakers is discerned as the ocean beats with fury upon the outer edge of the massive reef. A narrow brown line gradually coming into view, marks the belt of shallow water, a couple of hundred yards wide, covering the surface of the reef between the breakers and the white beaches of pure coral sand which border the little islets on the reef. The houses of the natives, picturesque and cool, soon peep out from the thick green cocoanut groves. Walk straight through these groves for 150 to 300 yards as the case may be, and you will have crossed the island and find yourself in face of the deep blue water of the lagoon, with another intervening brown belt of shallow water similar to that on the ocean side of the reef.

The reef which encloses the Milli lagoon is still bare, at intervals, to the extent probably of a third of its area. Rarely are these intervals fordable on any lagoon reef as the sea rolls over them freely into the enclosed area. On the other two-thirds of the Milli reef the ocean has formed, from coral *débris*, many islets varying in length but seldom attaining 300 to 500 yards at their greatest breadth. So near the level of the ocean and covered with stately palms whose crested heads tower above the few trees that find a home among them, the islets scattered on the reef between the deep blue ocean on the one side and the deep blue lagoon on the other, lie like a chaplet of emeralds set in a sapphire sea. The beauty of the coral gardens formed in the clear pools on the seaward face of a reef has been often described. Assuming every shape of miniature shrub and tree and with fish of dazzling colour and varied hue darting to and fro among the branches, these fairy-like gardens, once seen, can never be forgotten. But they are not common, and can only exist in clear deep pools with a perennial supply of the freshest and purest seawater pouring into them.

The narrowness of the land makes the climate of these islands cool and, for a tropical latitude, delightful. Truth compels me to add that thing of beauty though it be, a lagoon island has drawbacks even from an æsthetic point of view. There are no hills, no valleys, no running streams, no land birds, very few flowers and none of the features which in other lands stimulate the imagination and make life beautiful. The effect is shown by their barrenness in tradition and legend so plentiful among the same races inhabiting high volcanic lands.

In his natural state, the wants of the lagoon islander are few. For food there is always the cocoanut, and in the larger islands the breadfruit and Jack fruit; while all have the Pandanus of which the natives are extremely fond. The singular cones of the Pandanus are chewn for the sweet juice, or the substance, extracted by maceration, is formed into long bands which make a not unpleasant confection. The sea and the lagoon abound with fish, tasteless and insipid to the inhabitants of a colder clime but regarded by these people as delicious and often eaten raw when caught. They have their feasts of turtle and, on the whole, lead a joyous, contented life, marred only by failures in the cocoanut crop, by the tyranny and cruelty of a chief, or by the ravages of fell disease.

For dress they delight in gaily-coloured, well-made mats, or rude kilts of cocoanut or pandanus leaves. Their taste for decoration is shown in the necklaces and belts made of innumerable rings sometimes wonderfully minute, cut out of cocoanut-shell, highly polished and sewn on cord made of the cocoanut fibre. To the necklaces a large disc of burnished tortoise-shell is often attached and the native "masher" is then complete. Men wear the hair long, and in some of the westward islands tied up in chignons of such size that, but for the thin beard and moustache, it is impossible to avoid mistaking them for women. The women, on the other hand, often let their hair hang loosely down. This long, straight hair is characteristic of the Polynesian. Of the Papuan race, with its crisp, wiry hair, I saw no sign on any of the lagoon islands. In all, the hair is thick, straight and generally coarse, but in some cases so fine as to suggest a Hindoo strain in the blood, especially where accompanied by the light form and delicate hands and limbs often characteristic of these islanders. The lobe of the ear is a special object for decoration. Gradually enlarged from childhood, it hangs on each side of the face in a long thin ring reaching to the level of the chin. In full dress, a green cocoanut-leaf is curled and distends the ring, and forms the favourite ornament in use among the *élite* in the western islands.

Such is the lagoon islander in his natural state. Civilized, his desires expand and wants increase. Among the women, artificial flowers, fashionable hats, and high-heeled boots come gradually into use. The men eagerly barter their copra for biscuit, preserved meats, tools or implements, adopt European clothing and in other ways conform to European and American usages, on the acceptance of which the missionaries of both nations seem to me to set unwise weight.

Civilized or uncivilized, the water question must become a serious one on these low flat islands. Ponds are dug out of the coral rock or hollows cut in the cocoanut-trees and the rain is collected in them. The rocky ponds are also used as bathing-places and the natives drink the water without, it is said, suffering the ill effects which a European would anticipate.

Groups of all ages and both sexes may be seen disporting themselves in these stagnant pools and occasionally one of the number will sweep the scum from the surface and drink a handful of the dirty tepid fluid below. Some day, fever and dysentery will avenge poor outraged nature but no instance of mischief has yet been known. The purifying character of the limestone may have something to do with past immunity, but the conditions of life—the food, clothing, and personal habits—have within the last few years much changed among these people. Their chief drink has hitherto been the cool and bright fluid contained in the green cocoanut; but the enormous numbers so used materially affected the production of copra, only to be made from the ripe nut in which the fluid is neither so abundant nor palatable. Hence, the use of water is becoming more common and the erection of cisterns to hold a proper supply will be one of the first economical and sanitary reforms to be undertaken.

The water question becomes serious also for vessels cruising through these lagoon islands. European traders living upon them take care to have the roofs of their houses covered with galvanized iron, and catch the rain-water as it falls; but the quantity collected is only enough for their own use, and they have none to spare for the supply of shipping. As one gazes on the merry crowd sporting in a dirty, stagnant pool, visions arise of the old navigators, from Magellan to Roggewein and Anson, who endured through two long centuries terrible privation in crossing this great sea. No wonder they dreaded these low and incomprehensible islands. Their unsheathed, worm-eaten ships and their scurvied, perishing crews could find neither help nor health on these waterless shores. Knowing nothing of the openings which often lead to splendid shelter within the lagoon, the old mariners sought in vain for anchorage. They learned to dread these islands and, unhappily, were not aware of the magnificent high volcanic islands with fine harbours, pure fresh water, and abundant herbs and fruit, that would have saved from death the thousands with whose bones the bed of the Pacific is widely strewn.

My picture of life among the atolls is not, I fear, altogether inviting. But they have their pleasant features. The climate in most cases is bright, dry, and delicious: the beaches are beautiful and a constant inducement to sea bathing; and the facilities for fishing and boating very great. These are their only natural attractions, but it is marvellous to see with what charms taste and refinement can adorn a home even on one of the narrowest of these little islets. Let us take as an example the lagoon of Jaluit, the German metropolis of the Marshall Islands.

The Jaluit lagoon is a very fine one about forty miles long and twelve miles broad. The entrances are wide and easy and the anchorage is abundant and safe. A great navy might find convenient shelter at Jaluit and that, I presume, was the reason for its selection. The surrounding reef is exceptionally barren of dry land. I doubt if a full seven-eighths is not under water, while the islets on the remaining eighth are of such small area that they cannot contain altogether more than 500 to 600 acres. On one of these little islets, not more than ten to fifteen acres in extent, the embryo capital is built. Opposite to it were anchored seven schooners and cutters employed in the inter-insular trade, while a large bark and schooner were loading for Hamburg with the produce which the smaller craft had collected.

A great board, on which is printed in large

letters "Kaiserlich Deutches Protektorat," is the first object that strikes one on entering the little Metropolis. The town consists of two rambling, low-built wooden public-houses of the old colonial kind, two capacious wooden stores indicating the extensive trade of the German firms to whom they belong, and three or four adjacent dwelling-houses, well built and commodious and occupied by the managers and people connected with the stores. The only other building is the unpretending residence of Dr. Knappe, an able and courteous gentleman from Samoa who administers the government of the Marshall Archipelago. The rest of the little islet is given up to the everlasting cocoanut and pandanus which flourish with their usual luxuriance on the sandy soil. The natives in the whole lagoon are few. Scarcely any live in the metropolitan islet of which the land is not more than twelve to thirteen feet above the level of the sea.

On this unpromising spot a small Paradise has been created. To those travellers who have enjoyed the hospitality of the gentleman representing the firm of Hernsheim and Co., and of his accomplished wife only a year or two from Germany, Jaluit must be a green and pleasant memory. Music and painting lend their charm to the interior, and the hand of taste is visible everywhere. The carefully cultivated garden already abounds in tropical shrubs and flowers and will soon be productive of the best tropical fruits. The tame pigeons cooing from the dovecote and the little cow grazing quietly on her patch of freshly planted grass, are homelike and pleasant to those who have wandered, as we had wandered, through so many of these monotonous atolls.

Not the least striking feature at Jaluit were the four white Australian cockatoos, tamed by a gentle hand, flying at will from shore to ship and from ship to shore or clamorously appealing for the notice of their mistress on the verandah or the little lawn. And all this on land so limited that a short walk of a couple of hundred yards across the level garden carries one from the house, built near the edge of the quiet lagoon, to the opposite side of the islet where the loud-sounding sea sends its white breakers chasing each other ceaselessly to the shore. On that side a delightful little summer-house has been built. There one may gaze wistfully on the endless ocean and revel in its cool, refreshing breezes, doubly grateful

—let me add—because insuring temporary immunity from mosquitoes.

On another of the islets of the Jaluit lagoon, about a mile from the metropolis, a gentleman acting for an American Company at Honolulu has also established himself. He has only lately been joined by his wife but the hand of woman is manifest in the taste which one seeks in vain among bachelor houses in the lagoon world. That these islets, with all their natural drawbacks, are susceptible of such improvement is encouraging to those who look forward to the changes which increased facilities of communication must bring, and to the higher social life which the presence of refined women able to cope with the inevitable seclusion, cannot fail to create.

Have I succeeded in giving a clear conception of the curious little islets which form a Pacific atoll? I would fain hope so, but feel the very great difficulty of fixing in the reader's mind a picture so foreign to ordinary experience and so different to the conception I had myself formed. But, it may be asked, how do so many natives subsist on these islets and what resources have they to warrant a hope of future advance? The answer is easy.

They have in copra a trade capable of extensive development. They have pearl shell, tortoise shell and fibres of many kinds which may hereafter be exchanged for European food and clothing. They have also the *bêche de mer*, a sea slug much valued in China, and in the broader islets where the soil is deeper they have fine patches producing the banana, yam, and every tropical root and fruit. In such spots an indigenous taro, which they call puraka, is also cultivated, grows to a great size and is very nutritious and palatable. Their chief dependence, however, must always be on the cocoanut and pandanus, two of the grandest gifts of a beneficent Almighty to a tropical people.

Of the inhabitants of these islets I shall have more to say hereafter. They are a study too interesting not to have a chapter to themselves. Scarcely less interesting is the coral polyp, the humble means through which these marvellous atolls have been created. Secreting from the ocean the lime of which their minute frames are built, they lived and died leaving an innumerable progeny planted on the skeletons of their ancestors to continue the process till, in the course of ages, they formed gigantic bastions of limestone 2000 feet in depth, with a width at the surface varying from 500 to 1500 yards. The width at the base must be in proportion to the height and the gigantic size of the reef may be easily imagined. As it rises out of the ocean the insects perish, poisoned by the air without which we who inherit their work cannot live. On the narrow surface thus exposed, the gales and currents deposit *débris* and gradually form the detached islets surrounding the lagoon. Reference has been already made to the theories of alternate depression and elevation by which the peculiar formation of the atolls, with their inner lagoon, was explained till the discoveries of Mr. John Murray and Dr. Guppy in recent years. The question is still in dispute and naturalists must be left to decide which theory shall ultimately prevail.

On the lagoon side of the reef are caverns and cavities in which the large pearl oysters breed. Attached to the rock by their powerful beard at depths of five to fifteen fathoms, they adhere so firmly that a stout knife is often needed to sever their hold. The pearl shell is in itself valuable, and occasionally a rich pearl is found within. That for which her Majesty is said to have paid 6000*l*. to Storr and Mortimer, came from one of the Paumotu lagoons. Pearls of smaller size are frequent, but many must be lost by dropping out of the shells through the careless manner in which they are often opened.

The earliest records of Spanish conquest in the Pacific are connected with the pearl islands in the Bay of Panama. In 1517, only four years after De Balboa first sighted the great sea, Ponce de Leon caused timber to be carried across the isthmus and built a small craft with which to make the conquest of the pearl islands. The natives were cruelly treated and forced to give up 800 ounces of pearls found in their possession. They were further ordered to pay a yearly tribute of the same quantity. Of course this payment was impossible, as those found in their possession were the accumulated treasure of many years. They must have been as reckless as their descendants in opening the oyster, for the Spaniards afterwards discovered that many of the pearls were badly discoloured through the shells being opened by fire, a discovery which excited their just indignation at "the wicked carelessness" of the savages of those islands.

With its feathery palms, silver sands and glowing sunlight, with the heavenly blue of its waters and the peerless beauty of its fairy coral gardens, a lagoon island is a glorious thing to write about and to dream about. The temptation to go into ecstasies has often proved irresistible, but the prosaic skipper of a trading vessel regards the subject from a different point of view. Mere specks on the ocean, they are in his eye only dangerous obstructions. He must be for ever on guard lest in the darkness of the night the strong current send his ship amid the breakers which hurl themselves with fury upon the reef. The same strong current must be counted with if he find himself to leeward of the island at which he desires to call. Weeks may be spent in making fifteen or twenty miles so lost, and auxiliary steam will be invaluable as commerce increases. In entering or leaving a lagoon, the ship may also be imperilled by a sudden drop in the wind leaving her to drift helplessly on to the rugged, ocean-beaten reef.

To the colonist the extreme narrowness of the land, the shallowness of the coral soil and the absence of vegetable mould are incurable drawbacks. To the trader the attractions are great, and of island traders the German is becoming the largest and most active. Colonial merchants are doing what they can, but their capital is limited and they have need of it on their own shores. Official blundering in England has done much harm, but it will be worse if commercial apathy cause England to lose her dominant influence among the natives and leave them and their commerce to fall under German control.

The Milli atoll is a specimen of some hundreds on which great numbers of natives live. Wherever, from the depth of the ancient valley or the turbid character of the ancient streams, the polyp has been unable to flourish, openings are left in the reef wall and through them vessels enter the lagoon. Where no such openings exist a landing must be effected on the outer edge of the reef, the vessel meanwhile standing off and on at sea. For this landing natives are usually employed by trading ships and are very expert. A favourable moment is watched, and the boat pulled rapidly through the breakers. As she touches the reef the men jump overboard and run her as quickly as possible into the shallow and quiet water beyond. Cargo is landed or shipped in this way at the numerous islands which have no passage through the reef. The skill with which it is handled is so great that damage is rarely done.

On some of the islets sea birds abound, but they are the exception. One of the little islets on the reef of the Suwarrow lagoon is a curiosity in this respect. The small terns lie so thick that the visitor must walk with the greatest care lest he crush the eggs or the little ones, or kill the sitting hen who boldly eyes him and pecks and fights in defence of her nest or young. When the birds rise they darken the sky as with a cloud. The cock birds go fishing during the day and return at night with the spoil for the sustenance of their mates and families. A bird island is well worth visiting, and that of Suwarrow will probably be a great attraction if the lagoon is found suitable as a place of call for the future steamers between Europe and Australasia through the Canal of Panama or Nicaragua.

The formation of the raised coral islands will now be more easily understood. The lagoon, probably shallow from the first, has been filled up and the whole island raised perhaps 200 feet above the sea. The reef now forms the coast of the island. Its abrupt sides seldom

Coast Scene, Niuè, Savage Island.

offer anchorage and are remarkable for the great blow-holes, formed of old caverns still connected with the ocean. Through these holes each advancing wave sends the water in lofty columns, forming gigantic fountains which fall back in showers of foam and rainbow spray into the sea. The coast of Niuè abounds with these blow-holes, very beautiful when watched from the deck as one approaches the island on a quiet day.

On raised coral islands, the soil is usually shallow but with abundant patches of a richer kind, while the inland caverns serve to collect cool and pure water. The productions are therefore varied and comprise all capable of tropical growth. Of these islands Niuè is an excellent example; and the coast view of that island on a former page is a good illustration.

The luxuriant growth and rich verdure generally associated with the tropics are only to be found in the mountainous island surrounded by its coral reef, sometimes four or five miles distant from the shore. Marking past subsidence, this reef also forms an impregnable breakwater of the most perfect kind. Deep, broad channels run parallel with the reef on its inner side, often separated from each other and from the mainland by shallows only practicable at high water. Openings through the outer reef lead to safe anchorage, generally opposite to some large valley or broad flat at the foot of the hills.

In these high islands the shore reef, as that attached to the land is called, runs out in broad level ledges, dry or nearly dry at low tide and separated from the ocean reef by the channels before mentioned. At half-tide, boats and canoes sail easily over the shore reef and by this means easy communication is maintained. The low shores are studded thickly with cocoanut palms and the richest tropical vegetation, while the hills are clothed with tree ferns, breadfruit and forest trees, shrubs and flowers, in the wildest luxuriance and beauty. The soil is generally volcanic and islands of this kind are the most lovely and fertile of the tropical seas. Fiji, Samoa, and Tahiti are the finest specimens of mountainous islands in the Pacific, and only upon such islands is there a possibility of extensive European settlement. Even in them, settlement must be limited to planters and traders and skilled workmen, for the great mass of labourers must always be the natives themselves. The commercial value of these islands is considerable, and their military value equally great, for the natives are numerous and might be easily drilled and trained to become troublesome to the rising English colonies of Australasia. At present I doubt if half-a-dozen natives in any of them could be induced to fight against England on behalf of a foreign power; but the Polynesians are a tractable race and, once accustomed to a new order, would probably accept the position.

The mountainous islands abound in rich scenery, are abundantly watered, and teem with animal and vegetable life. The climate, delightful in the dry, winter season, is hotter, more moist, and more oppressive in the wet, summer season than that of the lagoon or coral islands. They yield every tropical product in the highest perfection and their staples are sugar, coffee, tea, spices and tobacco. All of these are superseded, for the present, by the cocoanut, which grows admirably on the coast of the mountainous islands, but of which the low coral islands are the natural home. The cocoanut gives the valuable copra to Europeans. To the native it gives food and drink and affords material for his clothing, for his canoe, his house, and all domestic needs.

Copra is largely sought by Hamburg merchants on whose trade the much-talked-of German interests in the Pacific are based. No German mission, no German exploring expedition, no German sacrifice of any kind for the benefit of the natives has accompanied their trade in copra. On commerce alone can Germany rest her claim. Commerce sounds well, but call it business and the odour is less sweet. Visions of natives duped, of base Bolivian dollars made island currency and of hard grinding in all directions, rise at the name. This is surely no fitting foundation for a great nation's claims, nor justification for high-handed measures such as have been adopted by Germany towards the kindly, English-loving people of Samoa.

The influence of England, of America, and of France has been bought with the blood of martyrs, the work of missionaries and explorers and the friendly and constant intercourse of their people with the islanders of the Pacific. Of these three nations England, in the extent and strength of her influence, is supreme. English is the only language which the natives know besides their own. Even in Samoa and in the Marshall Islands, the transactions of the German firms and their law deeds must be in English, which adapts itself to a "pigeon" form more readily than any other tongue.

Taught by English and American missionaries, serving in English and American ships, or working on colonial plantations, the natives have become thoroughly English in feeling and there are few islands in which "pigeon English" is not to be heard. The kindly intercourse of a century has borne fruit, and from end to end of the Pacific, whether still independent or under the flag of France, Germany, or Spain, the natives would by an immense majority "belong Peritane" (belong to Britain) if a voice were given to them in the matter.

Let Germany by all means do her share in the civilization of the Pacific. She has ample work for many years in the Bismarck Archipelago and in New Guinea. But why was it thought necessary to send an English plenipotentiary to Berlin and make with Germany mutual declarations for the recognition of each other's influence within a given sphere?

Germany's influence is bounded by her copra trade and the cruising-ground of her ships of war. The influence of England is a great and glorious fact, resting on the good-will of the native people, pervading the whole Pacific, and no more needing recognition from any other Power than does the sun shining at noonday over its broad waters.

CHAPTER III.

PAST AND PRESENT.

Spain's lost position—The old buccaneers—First missionary ship—French acquisitions—The whaling era—The kidnapping period—Peruvian kidnappers—English kidnappers—The sandal-wood era—Bêche de Mer—Pearl divers—Cocoanut oil and copra—Rich tropical products—Missionaries, traders, and natives—The innocent savage—The fate of Benjamin Boyd—Some innocent murders—A marvellous monarch—Dr. Dana at Fakaafo—Changed habits—Eccentric hats.

IN the Pacific the two widely differing systems of European colonization are again face to face. The Romaic, with its spirit of centralization, is represented by France and Spain. Additions to territory aggrandize their Governments, but extension of the field for individual enterprise seems a secondary consideration. The Teutonic, with its inherent tendency to decentralization and reliance on individual action, still finds in the Englishman its leading representative but running the new race with the German instead of with the Hollander, the Dane, and the Swede. The German will be a competitor far more formidable than the Spaniard or the Frenchman; but who can doubt that it will be in the Pacific, as it was in the Atlantic, and that the Englishman is bound to prevail?

Australia and New Zealand, the only great temperate countries, are occupied by communities that must become important nations. The power of the United Kingdom, backed by them and by the universal sympathy of the native races, is too solid to be shaken. Foreign annexations may continue and our Foreign Office blunder its best, but there is no room to found new nations in the Pacific. The great American people and the young nations of South America bound the ocean on the east. On the west we shall probably hear from China and Japan and assuredly from Russia; but the broad central region must be British in race, nationality, and life. Tropical colonies, created by other European Powers, can only bear to those of Great Britain the relation that the West Indies bear to the United States or Canada.

Australia, with her wealth and great natural resources, has already three millions of people. She will soon be federated and in time become the home of a powerful people. New Zealand, with her grand coast-line, safe harbours, and inexhaustible supply of coal and timber, with the varied mineral wealth in her mountain ranges and the varied pursuits of her vigorous people, must also rise—a second England set in the silver sea—and become a harder nut than distant nations will care to try their hands at cracking.

The time is comparatively recent when Spain predominated in the Pacific and shared only with an occasional Dutch navigator from the East Indies the honour of discovery on which her claims still depend. One of her sons was the first to behold the Pacific and gave a new ocean to the world. Magellan, in her ships, opened the passage without which easy access to the Pacific was impossible. De Loysa, Del Cano, Salazar, Saavedra, Hurtado, Grijalva, and above all, Mendana, endured the most severe hardship and displayed the greatest heroism in the exploration of the new sea. Saving our own Drake and Cavendish, nearly all the sixteenth century in the Pacific is connected with Spain. The end of the century had come before Ollivier Van Noort made the first feeble attempt on the part of Holland, to be quickly eclipsed by De Quiros whose further discoveries gave new lustre to the Spanish Crown. After Van Noort, came Spielberg, Schouten, Le Maire, Hartog, and Tasman. They, with a few minor navigators, made new discoveries surpassing in ultimate importance the Pacific discoveries of Spain. New Holland long bore witness by its name to the work of these old sailors. New Zealand and a host of minor islands bear still the same witness to their hardihood, enterprise, and suffering.

Spain rested content with her settlements in America on the one side and in the Indian Seas on the other; but Cowley and the brave old Dampier, Cavendish, Woods-Rogers, and other of the English buccaneers soon appeared to dispute her arrogant pretensions to exclusive trade and possession. They lay in wait for the treasure-ships which traversed the Pacific between Mexico and Manilla, and they harried her rich colonies along the Western American coast. With Anson's marvellous voyage and rich plunder we see the ending of the old era and the beginning of the new. The advancement of science and promotion of commerce were the objects of his successors—Byron, Wallis, Carteret, and Cook—names with which English settlement in the Pacific will for ever be identified. France, too, became active, and De Bougainville, Marion, and the unfortunate La Perouse left their mark on the eighteenth century.

Botany Bay had been settled but a few days when La Perouse lay in Port Jackson. Ten years later, in 1798, the *Duff* carried the first small band of English missionaries for Tonga, Tahiti, and the Marquesas. To tell how the Pacific and its islands have since been explored and occupied, would require more space than we can afford. Four centuries have not yet passed since the existence of the ocean was unknown. Scarcely one century has passed since the first small English settlement, and already the commerce of the Central Pacific attracts the notice of the world. Already are established on its shores energetic, self-governing colonies, full of vigour, and eagerly pursuing their great object—the building up, by God's will, of educated, prosperous, and contented nations.

Fortunate has it been for mankind that the Spaniards were thus superseded. Plunderers, and not workers like the gold-seekers of our day, they gathered gold and silver in great masses but only to minister to the vanity of the few into whose hands it fell. The privateers and buccaneers who hunted the Spanish galleons did the world a notable service, for they put into circulation the precious metals that would otherwise have figured only as plate or ornaments in the palaces and churches of Spain. The Philippines, the Pelews, and the Ladrones with a few other islands on the edge of the Western Pacific, still belong to Spain, but in the great ocean itself her possessions are confined to the Carolines. Her priests made an heroic attempt 300 years ago to Christianize the natives of the Carolines and suffered martyrdom. Since then nothing has been done by Spain in the Caroline Archipelago which lay utterly neglected till Germany took possession of Yap, the most westerly island of the group, in 1882. The resolute resistance of Spain and the arbitration of the Pope on that occasion are events too recent to require more than passing reference.

France has acquired in the Western Pacific the large but infertile island of New Caledonia, and the group of Loyalty Islands. In the Eastern Pacific she has the beautiful Tahitian group, the Paumotus, Marquesas and many other islands. Not the least important is Wallis Island, the seat of a Roman Catholic bishopric, with a cathedral, a convent and schools in which a considerable number of natives are trained as missionary teachers for the other French islands.

Germany has only lately entered the field. Through Hamburg enterprise she has acquired in the Western Pacific large and valuable tropical islands, the Bismarck Archipelago, part of New Guinea, and all the Marshall group. Her hand is also on Samoa and thanks to the inertness of England is not likely to be removed. Probably not one in a hundred of the Samoan people desire to be German, and the remaining ninety-nine would eagerly become English if the chance were offered to them.

Different epochs clearly mark the later history of the Pacific, and of these the whaling era was most important to the native people. In the days before gas and kerosene superseded fish oil, large whaling fleets were fitted out from England and America, and a few ships were sent from France. The young Australia also contributed her quota to these ships which frequented the Pacific in large numbers in the last decade of the eighteenth century. The natives shipped as sailors and returned to their homes talking English " as she is spoke " in the forecastle of such vessels. Runaway sailors began to settle among them, often men of fair character escaping from tyranny and ill-treatment on board and doing much good among the natives who were in manners, morals, and knowledge, far inferior to these Europeans. The good which the natives derived from whalers far outweighed the evil, and to the intercourse of whalemen is due the breaking down of savage barriers more than to any other cause or people.

Escaped convicts from Australia soon made their appearance among the natives. They were a desperate and dangerous class from whom as a rule no good could come. Happily there were exceptions, men of better character expatriated for poaching and minor offences and escaping at the hazard of their lives from the cruel brutality of a convict *régime*. Happily, too, the worst of these men were short-lived. They killed each other, died of their own debauchery, or were killed by the natives, the usual end of such men and well illustrated by the history of the mutineers of the *Bounty*.

A kidnapping era followed and is connected by the natives more especially with Spain. This is partly owing to traditions of the older time when Spanish ships forcibly took western natives in large numbers to repopulate the Ladrones and the other islands whose inhabitants they had worked to death in mines, or wantonly slain. It is more due, however, to the rascally modern kidnappers from Peru, between whom and Spaniards the natives know no distinction. Englishmen have kidnapped and fought, and have done regrettable work as well on the African coast as in the Pacific sea. But the Peruvian kidnapping, about five and twenty years ago, was marked by a callous brutality peculiarly its own.

Landing armed on one of the little lagoon islands, these ruthless scoundrels would sweep off all the people worth removing, and leave only the helpless aged and the young children. Taken to Callao for the plantations or sent to the guano islands on the coast, many of these people must still be in Peru. At Niuè I spoke with an old man, the surviving brother of two of these kidnapped men who escaped together from Callao. One died, and it was some years before the other contrived to get back to his home at Niuè. The vessel by which he was first kidnapped was full of natives, and had probably 200 on board. Disease broke out on the voyage and the greater number died before she arrived at Callao.

The lagoon island of Penrhyn also suffered greatly. The people are a fine manly race of the true Maori type, speak the Maori tongue and are as ready as Maoris to fight when required. Dangerous to attack, they were deceived by false promises into taking passage for a neighbouring island. Nearly all the people on Penrhyn took advantage of the opportunity and when thus decoyed on board were battened down and taken to Callao. The rest of the inhabitants were away getting *bêche de mer* on the reefs, and returning to the island found none but the old and helpless to greet them. For many a day they remained ignorant as to what the fate of their relatives had been.

Fakaafu, Nukunono, and Nukufetau have the same tale to tell. When the natives were likely to resist, they were decoyed. When too weak to resist, they were seized and torn away. Some of the Nukunono natives were at Wallis Island working for the Roman Catholic Mission, and returned to find their homes deserted and their relations gone. They had themselves been converted to the Roman Catholic Faith and their descendants are to this day the only exclusively Roman Catholic inhabitants on any of the islands around them.

At many of the eastern islands similar stories were told me, differing from each other only in shades of brutality. The Peruvians were materially helped by "Kanakas," a name given to the natives after a word in their own language merely signifying men. As far back as 1859 many of these Kanakas, having deserted from whaling or trading ships at Callao, were serving in the Peruvian navy. There are black scoundrels as well as white and it would be odd if the kidnappers did not find among these half-savage Kanakas tools only too ready to show the way—especially to those islands peopled by tribes who had been their hereditary foes.

The Kingsmill and the far western islands, with large and more warlike populations, were regarded as dangerous and the kidnappers of the Peruvian epoch kept clear of them. But in these islands, as well as in other groups, I found the English and colonial kidnappers had been at work in later days. More than once I was accosted in broken English or Fijian, and learned from the native how his canoe had been run down—accidentally of course, the kidnappers would say—and he and those with him taken on board. Or, as more frequently happened, how the white man had made presents to his chief or king who ordered him to go with the white man wherever he might choose to take him. But in no case did I find the least ill-feeling exhibited. They were treated well on board and spoke of the kindness shown to them on the plantations where they worked. They had been sent back with wages which to them represented great wealth, were proud of their English, and as ready to "belong Peretané" as the rest of the people in these seas.

The sandal-wood trader was another important personage who played no small part in the Pacific in his day. Old, dilapidated ships, well manned and well armed, were employed for this dangerous work. Peter Dillon gives an excellent description of sandal-wood trading, in the rare and interesting account of his own experiences in the early part of the century, prior to his discovery of the remains of La Perouse. The mountainous islands which produce sandal-wood, are populous, and the natives generally among the worst of the savage Papuan race. Bargains were made with chiefs to cut and deliver the rough logs which the traders trimmed so that only the heart of the tree should go to China. The ships engaged in this trade were from India or Sydney and the profits were enormous. The sandal-wood cost on an average 10*l.* to 12*l.* per ton, and was sold for 60*l.* to 70*l.* in China. Fortunes were made by a few shipowners in this trade and the earnings of the men were large, but it was probably the least beneficial to the natives of any in which they engaged. Chiefs would dispute the right of ownership in those by whom the wood had been cut and sold. Or they would endeavour to murder and rob for the sake of plunder, as savages will mostly do. Hence war to the knife was common with those engaged in the sandal-wood trade and none but old ships, only fit to carry timber, were risked in the adventure. This trade lasted beyond the middle of the present century, since when sandal-wood has become more scarce and the quantity obtained comparatively small.

Bêche de mer was another prominent source of traffic in the early days. This ugly sea-slug (Holothuria) is a favourite soup condiment with the Chinese who term it Trepang and believe that it has great restorative qualities. Chinese junks have from early days traded for trepang with New Guinea. In the western groups it soon became the "Beachcomber's" best resource. Any runaway sailor, supplied with a large iron pot for parboiling the slug and able to muster a sufficient number of natives with their canoes, could go into the business. Rough sheds were easily put up with trenches dug across the floor to hold the fires for drying and smoking the Bêche de mer after it had been parboiled. Incessant watchfulness was needed in the process, but the capital required was trifling, and the skill to discriminate between the many qualities soon acquired. The Bêche de mer trade has now fallen into insignificance. The natives prefer to devote the little energy they have to spare to the preparation of copra, the most congenial of the employments in which they engage.

Pearl-shell in large quantities and of considerable value, has always been and is still a product of the Pacific lagoons. Nearly fifty years ago Commodore Wilkes, in the account of his exploring expedition, refers to the large quantity sent from the Paumotus, worth then only 9*l*. to 10*l*. per ton. Pearl-shell is now in use for purposes then unknown and the price ranges from 60*l.* to 100*l.*, while larger quantities than ever are exported. The difficulty is to get good divers. The diving dress has been tried by Europeans, but the uneven rocky bottom and the oysters' habit of breeding in caverns or hollows, renders the dress unsuitable. Native divers are indispensable and they come chiefly from Manihiki and Penrhyn. Their skill is proverbial. They well earn their wages but require long rests at intervals, and cannot stand the work of diving for more than a few years altogether.

Pearl-shell and all other products, even sugar, coffee, and tobacco, pale for the time before copra which has replaced the cumbrous and costly cocoanut oil. Copra has only been known in the Pacific during the last fourteen or fifteen years. I have described how the preparation was introduced by Godeffroi and Company, the well-known Hamburg House who laid the foundation of the German interests of which we have heard so much in these seas. The introduction of copra changed the face of the oil trade and gave a new value to the low Atolls which are the cocoanut's natural home. The kernel of the nut is dried and sent to Hamburg where the oil is expressed and the refuse sent, I believe, as oil-cake to England. Whether the idea was original or not, Godeffroi's company did a great service to the natives and to the Pacific by the change they introduced and which, like all changes, was regarded at first with great distrust. The cocoanut loves the sea air and the salt spray and on these low atolls gets both to its heart's content. The absence of grass or other competing growths makes the cost of cultivation small. The cost of gathering the harvest is very little more. The fruit ripens on the tree, is collected and husked when it falls, and the kernel, after being dried in the sun, is cut up and loaded in bulk in the ship's hold. The natives are very skilful in the preparation of copra. I saw an amusing race between two small parties at Swain's Island to decide who could cut up most quickly a given number of nuts. No work is so popular with the natives and there is no other to which they take with the same zest or will.

Sugar, coffee, cotton, tobacco, and the usual tropical products must in the end outdo copra in value and play a larger part. But they are essentially products of the high islands, and not of a kind which the natives themselves are

Cocoanut Palm, Swain's Island.

likely to take in hand. Throughout a large portion of the Tropical Pacific, copra must for many years be king and assert its beneficent sway over the natives to whom it is so good a friend.

In the old days of cocoanut oil, bêche de mer and general wickedness, and of which such harrowing descriptions are often given, the natives were assuredly, not so innocent and the white men as assuredly not all so wicked as we have been led to believe. Living outside the highways of the ocean in places too small or too isolated to be the residence of European missionaries, the names of many good men—traders though they were—are still cherished. Captain English (an American, by the way) spent time and money in teaching the Rakahanga and Manihiki people handicrafts of different kinds. He supplied them with tools, and to him they owe their present skill in building and in many other useful arts. George Ellis, who is still living among the Manihiki people, has made them skilful boat-builders and sail-makers. Their fleet of boats is a pretty sight; all are of their own building and fitting. Many of these traders preceded the missionaries, gladly helped them and paved the way for their subsequent settlement—men, for example, like William Webb whom I met at Ponapè, who had been nearly forty years on that isolated island and of whom I shall have more to say hereafter. Yet between missionary and trader there has always been antagonism, originating in the evil character of a few men in Tonga and in the other large islands to which missionary attention was first directed in the early days.

At some of the islands, however—Niuè, for example—there is the kindliest feeling between missionary and trader. The Rev. Mr. Logan of Ruk, in the Carolines, is another gentleman to whom the same good feeling on the part of the traders is manifest. I was surprised to find that they regarded as an unusual act of missionary consideration his holding at Ponapè a regular monthly service for the white men and not confining himself exclusively to the natives. That missionaries have done noble work among the natives needs not my testimony. Of many missionaries the traders themselves ever speak with respect. But there have been and still are others with sympathies less broad, who appear to regard themselves as sent exclusively to preach to the heathen.

Surely the isolated white settler is also a man and a brother, and, if a lost one, so much the more fitting becomes an effort to restore him to the fold, so much the less excuse for passing him by on the other side. The feud between missionary and trader is an old one. The sooner it is healed the better for both and the better, assuredly, for the native in whose progress towards civilization the trader could give to the missionary efficient aid.

The stories which one hears of the natives themselves are not only interesting but show how strange have often been the misunderstandings on both their side and our own. They show, too, that while possessing many of the nobler traits of savages, the innocence and guilelessness attributed to them were always without foundation. Captain Cook found the Tongans so amiable that he called their group the Friendly Islands. The Tongans are the finest of the Polynesian race; yet they were all the time plotting the capture of Cook's vessels for the sake of the booty, and he left them in happy ignorance of his narrow escape. The late Judge Fornander of Hawaii, in his learned work, has given the literal native account of Cook's murder. The Judge was a high official and a very old resident in Honolulu and his authority may be implicitly accepted. He tells us that the natives do not hold themselves at all to blame for Cook's death. They say the quarrel was entirely owing to Cook's own carelessness and the carelessness of those about him as to native customs and feeling. But they admit with shame that their forefathers and their king had twice deliberated on the possibility of taking the ships for sake of the plunder. They say, further, that when the capture by force was rejected as impracticable, a plan was proposed by the queen and accepted by the people, to make the women play Delilah to these Samsons. Happily this plan, though tried, did not succeed.

Later on we have the unprovoked murder of Mr. Benjamin Boyd in 1851 by the Solomon Islanders who had murdered three French missionaries a few years before. Mr. Boyd was a well-known Australian pioneer, and conceived the idea of founding in the Western Pacific a great Papuan Confederation. For this purpose he fitted out and armed his yacht the *Wanderer*, of 200 tons, and attached to her as a tender the schooner *Ariel*, of 120 tons, laden with goods of all kinds likely to be valued by the natives. Mr. Boyd's objects were lofty and he had a great advantage in being able to hoist the flag of the Royal Yacht Squadron as one of its members. On the 5th August he made his first land in the Kingsmill group and after staying there some time proceeded to the Solomon Islands. There he arrived on the 6th September, coasted from port to port and everywhere met with a friendly reception. On the 15th October, before breakfast, he went ashore pigeon-shooting, and was accompanied only by a native lad. Both were treacherously murdered and a sudden and furious attack was simultaneously made on the unprepared yacht. The attack was repelled after a hard fight and much slaughter, and so ended poor Boyd and his aspirations for a Papuan Confederation. The story has been graphically told in "The Cruise of the Wanderer" by Mr. Webster, a friend of Boyd's who went with him and who is now among the oldest and most respected of New Zealand settlers. The sailors of the *Wanderer* and *Ariel* were almost exclusively natives, of whom Mr. Boyd, even at that time, had no difficulty in enlisting 57, mostly men who had already served in whaling or other vessels. No more unprovoked murder was ever committed by natives. Their sole object was plunder, but that is a very intelligible object in savages who still believe that they should hold who have the power, and they should keep who can.

Some murders that appeared at the time most horrible are seen to have been innocent when the facts are known. I heard about several of this kind from natives who took part in them or who were near at the time. Take an early incident in the splendid Ahrno atoll in the Marshall Archipelago, as an example. There I talked with men now speaking tolerable English, but who about the year 1862 took part in the deliberate slaughter of seven sailors landing on their shores from a whaleboat with which they had, it is now thought, deserted from an American whaler in one of the islands of the same Archipelago. The men were famishing for water. Under pretence of taking them to a pool, the savages managed to separate and spear them. The natives who did this were simply panic-struck, thinking the strangers must be devils who would kill them if not destroyed. Sorry enough they were when they afterwards found out, through better-informed friends and relatives from other islands, what these devils really were. Soon afterwards they gladly received a trader—Charlie Douglas an old man-of-war's man—who has lived among them quietly for the last twenty years. Luckily they had in old Charlie a sailor of the best type, a favourite to this day with naval officers, their pilot through the islands when needed and an equal favourite with all who are brought into contact with him. How invaluable the aid which such a man might render to the missionaries! Ask him, and he will reply that he would be only too glad but that missionaries and traders don't, somehow, pull well together. There is no missionary at Ahrno to this day.

At Apemana in the Kingsmills, Tem-Baiteke, father of the present king, on ascending the throne made a clean sweep of the white men in his dominions. They were but five and his reasons for their sudden slaughter are not clearly to be ascertained. It is an old affair and natives are not at any time very precise, but the only reason I could hear was that when heir apparent he had been jeered at by some of these white men. This does not, to my mind, accord with native ways and I am disposed to think, if the truth were known, that the white men would be found to have brought this fate by some more evil deed upon themselves.

Most curious of all illustrations on this point was the visit, in 1840, of Captain Hudson, and others of the Wilkes Exploring Expedition, to the island of Fakaafu. Of this visit Dr. Dana has given an amusing account in his work on the expedition. He tells us how they were the first white men the natives had seen, how the king rubbed noses with them, howled, moaned, pointed to the sun, hugged Captain Hudson again and again, presented them with mats and food, persistently pointed to the sun, and begged them to be gone. Had Captain Hudson and his party been less strong they would have met a different reception, for the natives really believed them spirits or devils and would have taken any means to get rid of them. They had come from the sun. Of that no man with eyes to see right straight behind the new comers could doubt. What could bring them to Fakaafu if it were not to rob or kill the poor people there?

Dr. Dana's account was so interesting that I took some trouble to find if there was any tradition of the visit. The Peruvian kidnappers pretty well cleared off the people alive at that period, but at last I fell in with an old man who well remembered the event—even to the stealing of the botanist's tin specimen box which my informant described minutely. He further pointed out to me a deep cut in a cocoanut tree made at the time to show the height of one of their strange visitors. The cut was over eight feet from the ground and there must have been some tall men in the United States' Navy in those days. The gods of the natives, described by Dr. Dana as one block of coral stone 14 feet high enveloped in mats, and a smaller idol dressed in the same way at its side, now form part of a fence surrounding the little square in which a Protestant and Catholic church, both under native missionaries, stand side by side. Of the beautiful young cocoanut palm which he also mentions as standing in the left corner and which I hoped to see in green old age, there is now no trace.

The change in the people since Dr. Dana's day is as wonderful as the change in their gods. They wear European clothing (more the pity), use artificial flowers, and are generally on the road to civilization. But most wonderful in some of these islands are the hats which the women have adopted. Their native ecclesiastical governors issued an edict that church-goers must wear hats to be respectable. Straw hats are made, but only for men. The women have patterns after the latest European fashion, which are brought to them by their missionary countrymen from the central islands of Samoa and Rarotonga, whither they are sent for religious training.

We could not account for the eager desire of the natives for our newspapers till we learned that it was merely to make from them these church-going hats. The paper is pasted together, sheet on sheet, till thick enough to form a narrow-brimmed, high-crowned head-dress. This arrangement, covered with coloured print and adorned with cheap artificial flowers, is highly prized and deemed fit for church or the very best society. The beauty of their hats is short-lived for they will not stand the rain. Being unlined, the inside is often a curiosity. In the crown of one I saw a likeness of Garibaldi surrounded by a mass of letterpress blurred by perspiration. In another, paragraphs of the *Rationalist,* an Auckland paper devoted to what it calls Free-thought, thought which however free is cer-

tainly not the literature one would select for the simple children of nature of whose existence we hear so much and see so little in wandering among these lovely isles.

CHAPTER IV.

SOME OLD-FASHIONED CELEBRITIES.

The trader of the old school—The trader of to-day—In the Majuro Lagoon—Bully Hayes—Hayes at Manihiki—His doings at Ujilan—To windward of his pursuers—Steals the *Lotus* at San Francisco—His exploits in the *Pioneer*—Renames her the *Lenore*—Future Hayes's impossible—Modern communications—Modern trading establishments—Samoa, Tonga, and Germany.

WELCOME harbours of refuge these lonely islands must have been to the wild knights-errant of the Pacific on whom so much good poetry has been wasted, and who are now happily no more. Can I in common decency pass on without reference to them and the dusky broods they loved to rear? The men who burst all links of habit, and who wandered far away from island unto island at the gateways of the day. How hard I tried to find them and how glad, when made familiar with their several stories, to learn that they had long since gone to—let us hope—a better world.

Paunchy Bill, Joachim Ganga, Paddy Concy, Joe Bird, and a host more of romantic ruffians and roving rascals, have left behind them names still talked of and the memory of deeds still recounted on many a lonely isle. Each in turn has died the death natural to such notorieties, but the depraved white man is still referred to occasionally in missionary reports and he has been revived with great effect for political purposes in the dispatches of Governors of Crown Colonies. In truth, the old knight-errant of the Pacific is dead and the quiet trader has taken his place. He, too, has burst all links of habit, has torn himself from friends and home, suffers privation, faces danger, and leads a life of isolation in order to earn bread for himself, or for others in some far-off land dependent upon him. But he looks forward to the time when he can resume old ways and return to well-remembered scenes, doing his work in the meantime faithfully and with a quiet heroism none the less noble that it is unconscious.

Only the best men among the older wanderers are now to be met with. Some, so old as to have abandoned all idea of leaving, are traders implicitly trusted by the merchants in other lands with whom they deal, and will die respected by the natives among whom their lives have been spent. Occasionally rough in manner and rude of speech, bearded like the pard and swearing as they used to do in Flanders, it is yet the sheerest nonsense to speak of their depraving natives who can only acquire from them habits and ideas better and higher than any they are likely to acquire from their own chiefs and kings.

I mixed freely with these men and saw them at their worst, that is to say, after the mild indulgence to which the excitement attending the rare arrival of a vessel sometimes leads. The drinking in itself was a mild affair, but I heartily wish that some among them would take a friend's advice, swear less and be more careful of speech. They are mostly old sailors with whom swearing is a mere bad habit and it is impossible to be much among them without appreciating the manly qualities which the rough exterior covers but cannot conceal.

I had heard and read so much against these traders that my prejudices were strong. I feel therefore the more bound to make this *amende* and to raise my protest against the slander of men who, while seeking an honest livelihood for themselves, are doing good service to their country and helping in no small degree the civilization of the natives among whom they dwell. The surviving traders of the old era are almost exclusively British, and the universal desire of the natives to "belong Peretane" is their best vindication.

The traders of the new era are of a different order to those of the old. Enlisted from all classes and of many nations, honesty is a leading requisite, as much as ever, for the positions of trust they occupy. Some exhibit educated tastes. On the shelves of one, an Englishman, I observed works in the higher mathematics and found they were his greatest solace. Nor shall I soon forget the new year's night of 1887, spent in the small but hospitable house of another of these traders, a German and the agent of a German firm.

We were in the Majuro Lagoon in the Marshall Archipelago, and therefore in German territory. The *Buster* lay at anchor in the lagoon and we had gone in a cutter to visit King Jibberik at the other end, twelve or fourteen miles away. On our return we called at Mr. Müller's, were pressed to stay the night, and gladly did so. We found at his house four traders met to celebrate the opening of the new year. Two were Germans, the third was a Scottish highlander, and the fourth an Englishman. The Germans were full of music, the Scotchman was all Burns and song, and the Englishman of no particular leaning that he suffered to be seen. With the simple accompaniment of flute and accordion these lonely traders passed the new year's night, and enabled us by their kindly welcome to pass it with them, —in a manner that none reading the absurd stories about Pacific Island traders could for a moment have expected.

Some of the Pacific celebrities of the old time were of a very different order. Captain Pease, for example, so happily killed by the natives at Bonin was no small personage in his day, but fell far behind his friend and associate Captain or—as he is universally called— Bully Hayes. From one end of the Pacific to the other the name of Bully Hayes may still be heard. I talked of him with many who knew the man intimately and whose accounts in the main were in accord.

"Hayes was a great, big-bearded, bald-headed man," said one of my Ponapé informants, "weighing 236 lbs., with a soft voice and persuading ways." He was an American, and must have been of what Americans call the magnetic type. Mad as a hatter at times, said one of the men who had sailed with him. For example, he had two favourites of whom he was very fond, the one a little wiry terrier he called "Barney," the other a big water-dog, "Dash." Pig-hunting one day, poor little Barney made some blunder. Hayes called him to his side and as the little dog looked up into his face shot him dead at his feet. Stung with immediate remorse, he threw the gun into the sea, went on board his little craft, smashed to pieces every article of furniture in the cabin and wandered about moodily, speaking to no one for nearly three days after. A volume would be needed for the stories related of this man, but they tell of a career so singular and happily so impossible of repetition that a short sketch will be interesting.

Hayes made his first colonial appearance about twenty-five years ago at Invercargill, in South New Zealand, as member of a small travelling musical company. Afterwards, as captain of a collier, he traded between Newcastle in New South Wales, and New Zealand.

During the Maori war he was strongly suspected of supplying the natives with powder and lead landed at out-of-the-way places on the coast. His practice, it is now known, was to stow the powder under the cabin and carelessly litter the floor with straw. No official visitor could dream that powder would be stored in so dangerous a place, while Hayes' request to be careful with fire was accounted for by the litter which there had been no time to clear away.

In New Zealand he contrived to buy the brig *Rona*, and made his Maori traffic easier by connecting with it a legitimate trade to Hokitika. The Maori war ended, Hayes started for Tahiti and began on new lines. The *Rona* foundered at sea near the lagoon island of Manihiki, where he was most kindly treated by the people who helped him to build another small craft. The little vessel finished, Hayes started in her with a party of Manihiki natives for a marriage feast at Rakahanga, an island distant about twenty miles. He took care to miss Rakahanga and ultimately found himself at Samoa. There he induced the hapless natives to engage for work on one of the plantations, not forgetting to charge their employer a good round sum for the expense he had been put to in bringing labourers to Samoa. "What an infernal scoundrel!" I could not help interjecting, as the narrative proceeded. "No doubt of it," said one of the party present, "but look at me. Hayes left me for five years on the little island of Ujilan to get copra for him. There were only a few natives and we made what copra we could, but he never came near me again. I was nearly dead, living on fish and cocoanuts and tormented with anxiety to get away. At last, by great good luck, a vessel called and rescued us. I never saw Hayes afterwards, but if he were to come here now and slap me on the back with one of his jovial laughs, and begin chaffing me about Ujilan, I won't say you mightn't see me shaking hands with him in less than ten minutes and ashamed to talk about being left at Ujilan any more."

"Well," I replied, "there is no accounting for these things, but in your case I should certainly have with him a very different settlement." "Ah," said my friend, "you didn't know Hayes, or you wouldn't talk in that way." I was happy to say I did not know him, and that, unless as governor of one of H.M.'s gaols, I should not care for the honour. My friend shook his head and told me that even such high people were not proof against Hayes. Look at the captain of H.M.S. *Rosario*. He was all over the Pacific hunting after Hayes at one time. Hayes happened to be at the missionary island of Kusaie when the *Rosario* called. He had just lost his own little vessel, the *Lenore*, close to that island, and had heard all about the *Rosario*. He went boldly on board, asked for an inquiry into charges which he was told had been made against him and also offered his services to pilot her into the harbour if they thought a pilot necessary. Then he contrived to get one of his leading accusers made drunk on board. The drunken man disgusted the captain of the *Rosario*, who was finally so taken by Hayes' ingenuous manner and abstemiousness (for he never drank) that he allowed him to go on shore on *parole* to bring off papers necessary for his defence. Hayes left in a small boat owned by a Kusaie friend. The friend returned with a sad story. The boat had been smashed on landing and he himself was badly bruised, as he showed. But poor Hayes, he thought, must have been stunned, for he sank and did not reappear. Nor did he reappear until ten days after the *Rosario's* departure. Then he took passage in a whaleship to Guam in the Ladrone Islands, where he got into trouble with the Spanish authorities and was sent as a prisoner to Manilla. At Kusaie (Strong's Island) he had been a rigid and pious Congregationalist, in great favour with the American mission there. At Manilla he became a devout Catholic, and through the representations of the Spanish priests was soon released and on his way to San Francisco.

At San Francisco Hayes contrived by some trick to get possession of a cutter yacht which he named the *Lotus*. The fellow evidently had poetry in him, with his *Lotus* and *Lenore*. He supplied her with stores by taking them without leave from one of the Californian lighthouses, and began a new career of adventure and rascality. The crew consisted only of himself, a native, and a Scandinavian named Peter, now living at one of the Caroline Islands near Ruk. They got to Jaluit, and one day after leaving that island, Peter was at the helm when Hayes in a violent rage went below for a pistol to shoot him. Arming himself with the iron boom crutch, Peter struck him down as, pistol in hand, he put his head above the companion. Then, without more ado, he threw Hayes and pistol overboard. He took the *Lotus* back to Jaluit, and reported what had occurred. She lay at Jaluit for some time, and was claimed and taken in charge by the master of a Californian vessel under power of attorney from the rightful owner in San Francisco. By him she was sold to a Jaluit trader and finally became the property of a native chief. As we entered the Jaluit lagoon I saw the *Lotus* lying upon the reef and fast going to decay.

Of Hayes' feats of roguery I heard everywhere. How he partly bought and partly stole from her French owner a vessel which he called the *Cruiser*. How he stole a cutter in Siam and voluntarily gave her as atonement to a man whom he had wronged, accompanying the gift with astounding accounts of her cost and quality. How he got into trouble at Samoa by using for illegal purposes the *Atlantic*, of which he was master. How he was made prisoner by the consul there to be dealt with by the first man-of-war, and how, instead of waiting for the man-of-war he took sudden passage for Shanghai in the *Pioneer* with his friend Captain Pease, a man as lawless and unscrupulous as himself.

This sketch of Hayes' career would be incomplete without giving his subsequent dealings in the *Pioneer*, for with that vessel he started on an entirely new course. The owners of the *Pioneer* were merchants in Shanghai. They had failed and the estate was in the hands of trustees. Pease knew this and concocted with Hayes a plot which proved successful. Staying behind at Bonin on the ground of ill-health, he sent the ship to Shanghai with Hayes in charge. The worst face was put on the vessel. Her copper was, to all appearance, destroyed, and she was made to look in every way as dilapidated as possible. The crew (Manilla men and other natives) were told by Hayes to protest against the vessel being sold or given up to the assignees till their wages were paid in full. Thus armed, he appeared before the assignees in Shanghai, and so frightened them with prospects of lawsuits and the probable cost of repairing the vessel that they let him have her for a nominal sum. Of this a very small portion was paid in cash. The remainder, it is needless to say, was never paid at all.

To re-engage the crew and repair the ship was an affair of little time. She was renamed the *Lenore*. Conversant now with all the affairs of the insolvent firm, he called at their various trading-stations at the islands, produced formal authority to wind-up their business and obtained from the agents what supplies of goods they had in store and what balances in cash they were able to pay. Among his victims on this occasion was Alfred Restiaux, now trading at Funafuti. From him and many others I heard the account now put together and which I believe presents accurately the strange compound of unblushing roguery, rough humour, and strong sentiment dashed with insanity which formed the character of this old Pacific notoriety, one whose like had not been seen before, nor happily can ever be seen in the Pacific again.

Men of Hayes' peculiar class could no longer find, even in the remotest parts of the ocean, a fitting field for their rascality. The natives are becoming well informed, the visits of trading-vessels more frequent and communication with the civilized world is rapidly improving. English mail steamers by way of the Cape or the Suez Canal, or San Francisco, connect through Sydney and Auckland with Fiji and with the chief central and southern islands of the Pacific. The Germans have a mail line of steamers connecting with many of their new settlements through Cooktown in North Australia. They have also a second line of large steamers, highly subsidized, which call at Sydney and there connect with Samoa and Tonga. The French have the " Messageries Maritimes " connecting at Sydney with New Caledonia and other of their Pacific possessions. The Union Steam Shipping Company of New Zealand, whose splendid steamers convey the monthly mail between San Francisco and New Zealand and Australia, send a branch steamer monthly to Fiji with which central colony both Melbourne and Sydney are also in regular connection. An Auckland firm, Donald and Edenborough, sends a regular mail steamer, under contract with the New Zealand Government, to Tahiti, calling at Tonga, Samoa, and the Hervey group on the way. Other Auckland firms send their sailing-vessels to different groups, while casual traders, old and new, go forth at odd times from Sydney and San Francisco, from Honolulu and Samoa. Vessels properly licensed and with a government agent on board, also make frequent visits seeking labourers for the plantations in Queensland, Samoa, and Fiji.

The Eastern Pacific is thus being put into regular and constant communication with all parts of the world. The Western Pacific, hitherto so secluded, will soon share in the movement. Colonial traders run from Auckland, and a Chinese merchant established in Sydney has lately opened a connection with some of the western islands from that city. An American company has taken up the business from Honolulu, and another firm has taken it up from San Francisco. British New Guinea is connected, through a steamer from Thursday Island, with those that convey the regular mails along the eastern Australian coast. German New Guinea (Kaiser Wilhelm's Land) is handed over to the New Guinea Company of Berlin for colonization and steamers connected with the direct German Mail Line will keep up the company's European communication through Sydney.

A wealthy and energetic Hamburg firm doing an extensive business with China on the one side and with South America on the other, has for some years been actively extending its operations in the Western Pacific. This firm does a large trade in the Bismarck Archipelago where it employs many small vessels and whence it sends considerable cargoes to Hamburg direct. Casual traders from other parts, even Chinese junks and Japanese vessels, find their way to these long-neglected western islands. Numbers of Arctic whalers, fitted out at San Francisco, go south to avoid the severity of a northern winter and make these western islands their winter resort. There is also the original German company, the "Deutsche Handels- und Plantagen-Gesellschaft Zum Süd-See Inseln zu Hamburg," which is far better known in the Pacific by the shorter sobriquet of the Long Handle Company. This great company has, in the Western Pacific, its agencies, coasters and large vessels loading for Hamburg, as well as its trade with Samoa, Tonga and Tahiti. The periodical visits of the American mission-steamer the *Morning Star* must not be forgotten; while the English mission-vessel *Southern Cross* does active work in the central or Melanesian region.

Movement has thus begun and will not be allowed to halt by the way. In a few years the Western Pacific will be as familiarly known as the Eastern, but its ever-increasing trade will—unless English merchants turn to it some of their energy and capital—fall under German control. Beyond the commercial question other considerations are involved. The political question is in a nutshell, and in this nutshell lie Tonga and Samoa. On them Germany casts a longing eye, and seems bent on their acquisition. Had I a voice in the matter, I should insist on the independence of these two important islands being preserved. Left alone they would—through trouble, no doubt, but none the less satisfactorily—work out their natural destiny. If intrigue is to render their independence impossible, at least let the natives say for themselves under what flag they desire to live. That it would be the English flag I do not doubt. So near to Fiji and to all the English colonies, I venture to say that we should at all costs resist the occupation of Samoa or Tonga, as military stations, by a foreign power. No one can begrudge Germany the large share of Western Pacific trade which Hamburg enterprise has earned for her. But mere trade interests can never justify a claim to islands which were closely associated with England and Englishmen many long years before Germany was heard of by the unwilling people whom she now seeks to force under her sway.

CHAPTER V.

A FEW PACIFIC ISLANDERS.

Passengers on the *Buster*—An "Ocean" Islander—The Eastern Islanders—Tongans, Tahitians, and Samoans—Origin of the races—Island characteristics—George Ellis of Manihiki—His early experiences—His account of Penrhyn—Description of Manihiki—King Apollo—Manihiki Turimen—Queer laws and customs—Old Rupè and the ghost woman—Maoris and witches—Religious observance—A contrast in native missionaries—The curfew at Manihiki—The *Gente Hermosa*—Missionary responsibilities.

During this cruise one of our troubles was fresh water, a trouble increased by the addition to our numbers of the shipwrecked men from Starbuck. Water is not to be had at lagoon islands. More than once we were put on short allowance, but the rain always fell in the nick of time and our cruse was never quite empty. The last occasion was just after leaving the Ebon Atoll. The padlock had been put on the water-tanks, but again the rain came in welcome downpour. All was stir and rejoicing. Tanks and tubs were soon refilled, cabin and forecastle busy with arrears of washing, and every available rope and spar was turned into a clothes-line. Among the people are some good specimens of the native races. Bill, from Rotumah, is a fine fellow, speaking English well and our favourite steersman when landing on a reef. Two other natives Turoa and Monakoa, are Penrhyn "boys," giants in stature and excellent pearl-shell divers. I watched them at Jaluit putting a sheet of copper on the *Buster*, each in his turn diving under the ship with a hammer and three nails till the work was done. Their longest time under water was five seconds, but they remain one and a half and even two minutes when getting shell at a depth of five to fifteen fathoms. Both speak broken English and they are identical in look and language with our New Zealand Maoris.

As deck passengers we had just taken from Namarik ten men and two women returning from a visit to their still heathen relations at Jaluit. They were themselves "missionary," under the American Mission and strictly obedient to its rules, one of which prohibits to communicants the use of alcohol or tobacco. The Namarik people were quiet, well-dressed and good-natured. They spoke more or less English and their political aspirations were to be relieved from Germany and to " belong *Morning Star*," the name of the mission-vessel which they used to designate America. They brought on board their own cocoanuts for food and drink, their own bottles of water and mats to sleep upon.

On Sunday these natives used frequent prayers and hymns in a manner so simple and unpretending as to prove them sincere. They were a pleasant, well-behaved and cheerful people. Nor were they in the least an annoyance though moving about in all parts of the vessel with a freedom that would have been very shocking to cabin passengers travelling with their own countrymen and countrywomen, under the same conditions, in any other part of the world.

These Rotumah, Penrhyn, and Namarik people are fair types of island natives in their several ways. But we had also on board a native from Ocean Island, taken up at Majuro to be landed at Pleasant Island whence he hoped to get back to his own little home. He had been working at Majuro, and spoke a broken English tolerably well. Tombu was the native name of this gentleman, but he was known as

Mr. Jones. His usual dress was a cotton shirt, and nothing more. It was his washing day also. The shirt was hanging up to dry, and Mr. Jones' wardrobe being exhausted he quietly promenaded the deck stark naked, and was not ashamed. His smiling face and perfectly unconscious air were inimitable, and luckily no ladies were on board. Mr. Jones told me that all the people on Ocean Island "dress that way." I should have said that Bill was a Wesleyan, the Penrhyn boys were Congregationalists of the English branch, and the deck passengers whom we left at Namarik belonged to the American branch of the same Church. Mr. Jones was still an unmitigated heathen, I need hardly say.

These people fairly represented the progress of the islanders in civilization. There are intermediate stages, but even the heathen almost invariably cover themselves now with European clothing or some other approach to costume.

To the eastward, where civilization began in the Pacific, they have made most progress. There the people are more purely Polynesian, light in colour, fine in form, and graceful and attractive in manner. They build good houses, wear European clothes, and are far in advance of the natives of the Western Pacific. The Papuans, at all times and in all places, have been cannibals. The Polynesians, with the exception of the Maoris and Raratongans and a few others, were not. Their general detestation of the practice is so marked as to suggest the thought that the Maoris and Raratongans may have grown to it by contact with the Papuan races with whom they came into conflict.

Passing over many hundred miles of ocean covered with islands occupied by races of mixed Polynesian and Papuan blood, with perhaps a strong dash of the Hindoo, one suddenly falls upon the pure Maori in the little lagoon island of Nukuor, situate in the centre of the Caroline Archipelago. The Nukuor language is Maori of the oldest and purest kind, easily seen despite the constant change in the application of words which is characteristic of uncivilized nations. I regretted that our stay at Nukuor was too short to enable me to make any inquiry as to their traditions, but learned that they too had never been cannibals. The population of Nukuor cannot exceed one hundred souls and quite likely they have lost all record of much of their past; but their presence in that isolated condition, surrounded by thousands of other race and tongues is strange and interesting. I was only able to observe that most of them understood a little English, that they have no king, that they were remarkably keen traders refusing to sell their copra except at impossible prices, and that they would not have a native missionary on their island. They did not see of what use he would be unless he could teach them English. I hardly needed further proof of their identity with our own dear but exceedingly plain-spoken and practical Maori.

The Tongans, the Tahitians and the Samoans —the Tongans especially—seem the purest specimens of the Polynesian race, and very noble savages they must have been. The Maori is apparently more mixed, but though rougher and ruder he is certainly not inferior in mental or moral attributes. The Fijians are more difficult to understand, for in them Papuan and Polynesian seem inextricably mixed. Their thick crisp beards, great moustaches and bushy heads of hair, are peculiar characteristics, and I have seen among them faces that answered exactly to the old sculptures of Assyria and Egypt.

Opinion as to the origin of the Pacific races is much divided. Some ethnologists hold that they are from the West Coast of America and identical with the Indians of that continent. The prevalent winds are appealed to in support of this opinion. Others assert that these winds, though prevalent, are not invariable, that language, tradition, custom and physical attributes, point to the west, and that India was the probable home from which they found their way eastward, even to America. If the latter view be correct, they must be a very ancient people and for many thousands of years have occupied their present isolated homes. At Satoan, in the Carolines, I saw the remains of a canoe of a construction entirely unknown to any of the natives. The work was superior, the canoe broader, and the supports for the seats were cut out of the solid wood. It had drifted ashore, and the trader who was an old sailor, felt certain that it was one of the great number cast adrift at Java during the eruptions in the Straits of Sunda in 1885. The canoe must have drifted at least 1500 miles to Satoan, not at all impossible when the strong westerly current is taken into account.

I have endeavoured to give a general idea of the islands with which the Pacific is strewn, but each order has its special characteristic. The mountainous islands have populations bright or gloomy, peaceful or warlike, kindly or savage, according to the scenery surrounding them and the circumstances under which they live. The raised coral islands have a population less diverse, but the atoll world and its people have a character little varied and peculiarly their own. Atolls are wonderfully like each other, and wonderfully unlike the rest of the world. Poetry and tradition find no congenial home in the flat little islets, so like each other in every essential feature. One of the most beautiful specimens of an atoll with one of the most charming people, is Manihiki, about 600 miles west of Tahiti. I had very favourable opportunities for learning the ways of these people, as we took from Auckland George Ellis, the trader to whom I have before referred, who had lived for years among them and was returning to his home with a Manihiki chief whom he had taken the round with him.

Ellis is a type of the old trader of the better kind of whom I have already spoken, a wiry active man, with features finely cut, with brain, energy and abundant pluck, and with the simple kindliness and honesty for which so many of these men are known. Occasionally he indulges in what he calls his jubilee. The term is borrowed

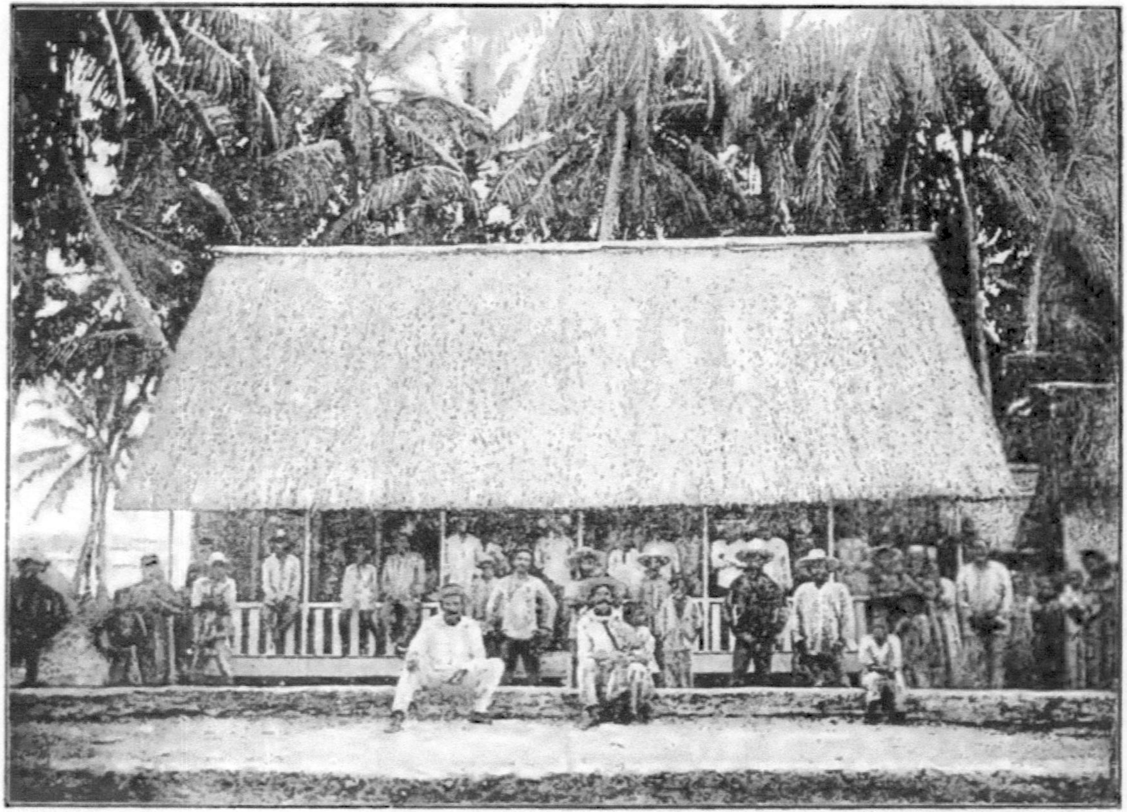

Copyright. Photographed by Mr. Andrew.

Ellis's House, Manihiki.

from the mission and indicates a temporary relaxation from their usually rigid rule. The first three days of May and January when the people meet together and pay their subscriptions for the service of the church, form this exceptional holiday.

Four-and-twenty years ago Ellis was a lad in Callao, wrecked in an English ship, on board of which he was a sailor. He shipped in a Peruvian vessel for the Eastern Pacific, seeking natives as labourers for Peru. They were taken for a year's service under contracts regularly signed and witnessed, but Ellis took a strong dislike to both the work and the men. So he stayed behind at the first chance which happened to be in Caroline Island, a small lagoon, where four men were fattening pigs on cocoanuts for sale in Tahiti. Caroline Island is about four hundred miles east of Penrhyn, to which latter place he afterwards went in a cutter of ten tons built by himself and the others on Caroline Island. At Penrhyn he found the natives in great trouble. They had been working in Tahiti and in Washington Island for Mr. Brander of Tahiti, and on returning home found their island depopulated in the manner I have already described. The natives said 3000 people had been taken, but the number must, in native fashion, have been greatly exaggerated. "It was not all grief, though," said Ellis; "they had lost friends and relations, but they had lost enemies too, for they were always fighting in those days."

The Penrhyn lagoon is about forty miles in circumference, and on the reef are many islets only a few feet above the sea and 250 to 300 yards broad. On these islets there were formerly eight different tribes, whose spare time was spent in quarrelling with each other. "The row," said Ellis, "was always about land or women, or the right of fishing and getting pearl shell in different parts of the lagoon." Feuds grew bitter, and parties would steal out, cut down the enemy's cocoanut-trees and walk off with his nuts. Sometimes there would be hard fighting and a good many dead be left unburied on the ground. But to their honour they never slew women or children. They made slaves of them instead.

Copra, pearl shell, and the missionaries, made a wonderful change. The two former made the islanders comparatively rich, the latter filled their minds with something better than fighting. But when Ellis went to Penrhyn, this happier condition had not been attained. As to the Peruvian kidnapping, the natives owed Mr. Brander money in Tahiti; so he complained to the French Government and their representation to the Peruvian Government stopped the kidnapping in that quarter.

The Penrhyn people soon learned to look to Ellis to protect them from future attack. They adopted him as a chief and called him Serikura, by which name he is known to the natives of many islands to this day. He taught them many useful arts, especially boat-building and sail-making in which they are very proficient. While he was in Penrhyn the natives became " missionary," gathered themselves together in two villages instead of being scattered among the islets, put up a church and school in each village, and obtained a trained native as their missionary. They have ever since lived peacefully, and are among the finest divers and boatmen in the Pacific. I saw a boat's way deadened when under full sail in the open sea, by one of the crew quietly jumping over the bows and hanging on till we, who were pulling, could overtake her. I saw quite enough at other times to convince me of the truth of the stories about their surrounding and driving shoals of porpoises ashore, and about many other daring deeds at sea. As my readers have not seen these things, I refrain from taxing their faith, and leave these and other extraordinary exploits to be recounted by some future visitor.

After a time, Ellis went trading to the more populous island of Manihiki, and finally settled there. He is very fond of the Manihiki people, though they have what he calls queer ways and queer laws. At opposite ends of the Manihiki lagoon, which has no entrance through the reef, there are two villages, each with its own king and each with 250 to 300 people. A neat white road of coral sand bordered with coral rocks and about half a mile long, runs down the centre of each village. The houses, very prettily built of white coral stone or of wattle well plastered with coral lime, nestle among the luxuriant cocoanut-palms on either side of the road, and being thatched the necessarily steep roofs add to the picturesque appearance of the scene. The churches of Manihiki are excellent of their kind, built in the same style as the houses but with pointed Gothic arches to the doors and windows, a form of arch adopted evidently because of the ease with which it could be constructed. The school is of the same style and, though roofed with iron, the

Copyright. Photographed by Mr. Andrew.

King Aporo's House, Manihiki.

steep pitch is preserved. In the interior of the church two spaces are railed off, one for the family of the native missionary; the other for that of the representative of the old family whose head formerly ruled them as priest and whom they now call king. The rest of the congregation sit promiscuously in their usual way on mats along the floor.

I knew our Maori King Tawhiao to whom his subjects pay fair deference, and I had known King Cakobau of Fiji whom none of his subjects dared approach except on hands and knees. I was therefore anxious to see what the king of a lagoon island is like and lost no time in paying my respects to his Majesty of Manihiki. Asking a native who spoke English to direct me to the king's house, he pointed at once to a fine-looking young man standing near the crowd assembled to welcome us on landing. "That fellow king," he told me, and, without further ceremony, shouted, "Aporo, Aporo, this man he want see you." Apollo smiled and drew near. We shook hands and made friends. Our intercourse was necessarily of short duration, but I had added to the list of my royal acquaintances that of the king of a lagoon island.

In the old days the priests owned no land, but were supported by the people. So the king has no land of any consequence now, but he has half the fines imposed upon sinners and offenders of various kinds. His income would be larger if it were not that these sinners are often of his own household. Custom, in such case, compels him to pay their fines which they can seldom do for themselves. An explanation of their system of government will make this anomaly intelligible.

The king, be it said, has no direct power. That has fallen into the hands of the native missionary whose holy office, combined with greater education and experience, makes him the real ruler of the people. The missionary, of course, has neither legislative nor executive authority. Both are vested in the Turimen or members of Parliament, elected yearly by the heads of households. The Turimen divide themselves into four committees who take alternate weeks of duty. They have no written law, and make no troublesome distinction between legislative, judicial, and executive functions. The native missionary pulls the wires, and the Government becomes in effect a simple Theocracy tempered by representative institutions. No distinction is drawn between offences which civilized communities leave to be dealt with *in foro conscientiæ* and those which they remit to courts of law. The legal offences are almost entirely in the nature of what we should call sins and leave to be punished by the awakened conscience of the individual, the reprobation of the community, or a higher than earthly power.

The Turimen declare the law, sit as judges and act as policemen. No formal trial takes place. Information is obtained as best it can be and the culprit merely ordered to pay the fine. Paid it will be, whether heavy or light, as the friends and family make it a point of honour to do so.

The saving feature in this queer system is that the Turimen, after handing over one-half to the king, divide the fines among themselves. Sometimes the fines are as high as five pounds, but that is only where women or wine have been the cause of very great offence. These and the breach of Sabbath observance are the subjects with which the Turimen have almost exclusively to deal, for thefts and crimes of violence are unknown. Where women are concerned, the parties offending are not only fined but drummed through the street of the little town from one end to the other. The drum is a wooden trough of the usual kind, but the native are skilful in its use and a very loud sound is obtained.

"This drumming," said Ellis, "is now a common affair. When they began it, the people who were drummed looked foolish; but now that they are used to it, the man and the woman, dressed in their best, go arm-in-arm before the drummer, laughing and joking with the crowd and even with the Turimen who can't help laughing, too."

Against drinking, or selling drink, the law is wisely severe. There is no reason why these natives should drink, for they have no poverty, no wearing anxiety, abundance of fresh air and all the food they require. Public sentiment is naturally with the Turimen in this prohibition, and there can be no difficulty in enforcing the law. But the methods used, which I shall presently note, go far towards creating a reaction. The Manihikians are indeed a kindly, amiable people, or these methods would have produced rebellion long ago. I was told that already the break-down has begun and that there are few, even of the Turimen themselves, who will not drink if they have the chance and if no other Turiman be nigh. They are full of humour and enjoy nothing more than tripping each other up. An occasion of this kind is a great delight, and affords chaff and gossip to the whole village for some time.

Sensitive to ridicule, as all natives are, they will resort to the most ingenious ways of averting it. I must tell, as an illustration, how my old friend Rupè, fattest and jolliest of Turimen, got out of a scrape one day. He had been on board a trading-vessel and taken a glass or two of rum—"very good rum," old Rupè said,—but, on getting into his canoe, found that though his head was right the legs had gone all wrong. How was he to face his friends on landing? Quick as thought, Rupè tumbled out of the canoe as she struck the little beach and, rubbing his arms and shoulders in the water, made believe to have a bath. Waiting till the coast was clear, he rolled up to his house unperceived and sent for the old "Ghost Woman," in whom the natives still religiously believe. She was a great friend of Rupè's, and by her incantations kept off all intruders till the evil spirit left him and sleep had restored his normal solidity and steadiness of gait. Thus was old Rupè saved from a heavy fine and, still worse, from the ridicule of his fellow-members and the village world. Speaking of the Ghost Woman, the faith of the natives in her operations is unbounded. They have also at this same Manihiki a favourite Wizard Doctor, who cures all kinds of illness by pulling yards of spun-yarn or baskets of old rags, out of the sides of the patient. Ellis has seen the thing done repeatedly and watched it closely, but has never been able to detect what he called, in colonial phrase, the swindle.

I remember, by the bye, once taunting an old Maori with their foolish belief in witchcraft. He listened attentively while I explained that we English were in the old time as foolish as the Maori and very cruel to helpless old men and women suspected of witchcraft, but that we had given it all up long ago.

"Yes," said my friend; "you stopped after you had killed them all. Why not let us do the same?"

I found it hard to reply. Nor shall I soon forget the Maori view of our behaviour, after the volcanic eruption at Tarawera last year. Upwards of a hundred Maoris, living at the foot of the mountain, were buried deep beneath the ashes. Other Maoris were employed by the Government to dig out their deceased friends and relations. Juries were summoned, and inquests held on the spot.

"A strange people you Pakeha," said one of the Maoris. "Everybody knows my people were killed by Tarawera; but you come here, spend much money, take much trouble, dig them out, talk plenty, and then bury them all over again."

The Government at Manihiki seems to the European much like a huge joke, but is really a great Godsend to these poor people. Healthy amusement of so many kinds is discouraged, and games and dances have been so rigidly repressed by missionary law, that their Government is the chief distraction left. They go to church five times on Sunday, and meet at stated times on weekdays to pray and sing hymns. But hear them talk in the intervals! Note the prurience of their minds, the absence of all delicacy and of what we should call respect for morality. Do this, and the conviction must be forced upon one that their religion and civilization are too often but skin deep. Who can wonder when reflecting that their welfare, spiritual and temporal, almost entirely depends on a self-sufficient, ignorant native missionary, of whose work the inspecting European missionary can, in the nature of things, see the outside only. The inspector calls at these isolated islands in the Mission vessel, sees the schools and people, finds all well dressed, demure, and looking well, stays a short time while his vessel beats on and off at sea, and then must hurry away to call at the next island. Great is the responsibility of those who train these native missionaries, for they copy the ways, adopt the ideas, and ape the manner of their teachers, with an exaggeration so extreme as often to make religion oppressive or ridiculous. At Atafu I saw one of these gentlemen dressed in ill-fitting black, with orthodox white necktie, creaking boots and white helmet, with Bible under arm and umbrella overhead, walking solemnly from his house to the church. The distance was about twenty yards; and his pompous look as he paced along, was most curious to see.

What a contrast was this to Kirisomè, a native missionary we afterwards met at Nui, another little lagoon island like Atafu. A fine, frank, open-eyed man, without pretension in manner or dress, keeping a vigilant eye over his flock but avoiding all mean ways in doing so. Kirisomè has guided the Nui people for nearly twenty years, and is a striking proof that the natives have in themselves good material for the work. All depends upon the training, and it is most unlikely that the same missionary could have turned out two such opposite specimens as Kirisomè and the gentleman at Atafu. At both of these islands, and at some of the others, the women wear the paper hats of which I have already spoken. They trip to church looking very prim and sedate, with their curious though well-shaped headgear topped with faded artificial flowers; but all of them happily still bare-footed. High-heeled boots, those atrocities of civilization, have not reached them to the present time.

I must return to Manihiki, which I take as an illustration of the general state of these lagoon islands though superior in many of the details. The laws are objectionable, and their modes of enforcing them, putting men and women in the public stocks or drumming them through the public street, are bad enough; but the methods of prevention and discovery which these Turimen adopt, are worse. If a Turiman suspect a man of having taken liquor, he will stop him at any time and order him to " blow " so that he may discover if his breath has lost its normal sweetness. The decision then come to is conclusive, adopted as a judgment by his fellow Turimen and the culprit fined accordingly. A "curfew" drum is beat at eight o'clock, and after that hour if any one is seen abroad the Turimen are down upon him with a heavy fine next day. Their lovely moonlight nights bring no enjoyment to these people. At Funafuti and other islands the Turimen go further. They march round the village during the night and quietly steal into the houses to see if all is right. It was found that the house-dogs barked and gave notice of their approach, so they forthwith decreed the destruction of all dogs on the island and again became masters of the situation.

How is it possible that self-respecting, honest men and women can be produced under such a system—especially in the absence of all healthy mental occupation or amusement? Can this constant *espionage* end otherwise than in making sneaks and hypocrites of one of the kindliest, pleasantest races on God's earth? The Manihikians are said to be the Gente Hermosa of old Quiros. They were heathen then and ought to be still more the Gente Hermosa now; but the whole system, and the rigid Sabbath observance are opposed to their instincts and contrary to their light, joyous natures. Already the cord is snapping. It is notorious that the Manihiki women are always seeking to leave the island, and that they have to be closely watched lest they should escape, when trading-vessels call there. Who can wonder that this should be? And if those who have the heart and the brains and the power do not find a remedy, who will further wonder if the reaction should grow stronger and the last state of these poor people be worse than the first, worse than the original state from which the devotion of many a missionary has so far raised them? In these distant lagoon islands where the population is so sparse and European missionaries with their families cannot dwell, the responsibility of those who send the native teachers to guide and practically rule these people is a responsibility of no light kind, for upon the native teachers, and upon their training and character, the future must depend.

CHAPTER VI.

SOME KINGS AND OTHER PEOPLE.

George Ellis gives his opinions—King Jibberik of Majuro—
  Jibberik's wars and conquests—Leilikè defies the
  Booboo-man—Jibberik's newest ambition—Leilikè's sad
  fate—A few other kings—Caste among the natives—
  King Tembainooke—His dominions and practices—His
  harem—Laziness unsurpassed and unsurpassable—
  Pleasant Island—Pleasant Islanders at deadly feud—
  A tour at Pleasant Island—How they fortify their
  houses—How they shoot each other—Europeans safe if
  out of the line of fire—Origin of the strife—Easily dis-
  armed—Introduction of the "Hellish" toddy—An old
  Pleasant Island trader.

MANY a talk about these people had I with my shrewd friend Ellis, both on the voyage and after he had returned to the bosom of his family—a handsome native wife and four fine children—at Manihiki.

"After all," to use his own words, "if they had not this church-going and turi-business to amuse them, what would the poor devils do? They never were a fighting crowd, but they had plenty of games and dancing and other amusements. Now, they won't even let a girl wear earrings, because the missionaries thought they must put down all that looked like heathen customs. I wish," he continued, "they could find some way of keeping their brains going. But they have enough to eat at any rate, plenty of fresh air, and no rent to pay. Now, in London, where I come from," added he, "there was many a thousand couldn't say as much. Look at this," and George held up to me one of the *Illustrated London News*, which I had given him on the voyage. The illustration to which he pointed was styled, "All that is left," and depicted a poor little half-clad Irish girl in Mayo, sitting amid the wrecks of the family furniture, before the door of a hut from which the family had just been evicted. "Talk of Manihiki ways," cried indignant George, "isn't that enough to make a man's heart bleed? You may tell me it's the law, but the chiefs of the biggest savages I know, wouldn't be chiefs long if they made laws like that. They may club or spear their people, but no one would stand their turning out and starving women and children, like that poor little thing there."

How could I answer my friend George? I had, myself, seen more foul poverty, more

The Majuro Lagoon is about twenty miles long and eight wide. The surrounding reef has the usual low islets dotted at intervals upon its surface. Generally they are about 200 yards wide, but in some places the reef is broader and the islets are wider in proportion. At one end of the lagoon they attain in some parts to even a mile in width. The population altogether is about 1000, pretty equally divided into two tribes of whom each has its own king.

At the narrow end reigned Jibberik, the name assumed by each successive monarch on ascending that particular throne. At the broad end reigned Kaipuke, also an hereditary title. Kaipuke owned bread-fruit and jack-fruit trees, possessed soil enough in some places for bananas and puraka, and had by far the best fishing-grounds. Jibberik, of the narrow end, had only cocoanuts, and looked with envious eye on his neighbour's richer dominions, greater power and wider renown. He contrived to pick a quarrel with Kaipuke; but not before he had quietly provided a stock of repeating-rifles, while the other side had nothing but the usual old-fashioned guns.

Jibberik showed consummate statecraft too.

Each kingdom had its boo-boo man who did all the oracle and augur business for the tribe, and who was held in the greatest awe and consideration. Jibberik learnt boo-boo for himself, and could soon plait and unravel cocoanut leaves and read the omens in other ways with the best of them.

He became in time his own boo-boo man and centred in himself both temporal and spiritual power. He did more, for he bought over one Capitamata who was Kaipukè's boo-boo man, and induced him to play traitor to his king and people.

So strengthened and forearmed went Jibberik forth to war. His troops advanced steadily in the native way; that is to say, at night they put a low stone wall across the narrowest part of the islet and slept under its shelter, being careful to fire their repeating-rifles with great fury in order to deter the enemy from disturbing their slumbers. At the dawn of each day they made another advance, killed any stray man, woman or child that came in their way, put up another stone wall, and gained possession of so much more of the enemy's country. All this time Kaipukè was kept in hand by his scoundrelly boo-boo man who declared the omens dead against him whenever he wanted to go out and fight.

At last Leilikè, one of Kaipukè's youngest and bravest chiefs, defied the oracle, and went forth with a few volunteers. The old men shook their heads, and they were right. Leilikè was soon brought back disabled by a shot in the groin. Could anything be more conclusive? The boo-boo man triumphed. Kaipukè felt the hopelessness of further resistance and made a treaty with Jibberik, exchanging dominions, surrendering his rich end of the island and going with his own people to the other.

This occurred about two years ago, and Jibberik, when I saw him, was regarded by his people as a great and conquering king. The scoundrel Capitamata had risen to be his boo-boo man and prime minister. King Jibberik is despotic, can at pleasure spear or otherwise slay any of his people who offend him, and is approached by them with due humility and awe. He rules with a firm and just hand (that, I believe, is the proper diplomatic phrase), and sternly upholds law and order, by which is meant, obedience to his own will and law. Only lately he speared to death a man who had dared to disobey one of these laws by picking a green cocoanut when the tapu had been placed upon them.

Thereby hangs a tale. Jibberik, with all his cocoanuts, bread-fruit, abundant fish and other wealth, is not content. He has lately bought a pretty little cutter yacht, the *Daphne*, of which he is very proud; but she has proved to him rather a dead weight and is rapidly going to ruin in his hands. The cutter cost 700*l.*, and in order to pay for her he was obliged to sell copra. The nuts must therefore be allowed to ripen and none be picked green for drinking purposes. Hence the tapu which put his people on short allowance and caused the untimely end of the lawless individual above referred to. It is a consolation to know that these natives, when they die or are killed, leave neither wives nor families unprovided for. The tribe and relations see to them as a matter of course, and this perhaps is one of the reasons why death is so lightly regarded.

Jibberik, with all his greatness, is still mortal and afflicted with rheumatism in the joints of the arm and knee. When I saw him he could not stand but was seated in the midst of his councillors on a mat on the damp ground. I ventured to tell his Majesty that a white man so

King Jibberik of Majuro.

treating rheumatism would be regarded as a fool, but I fear that habit is too strong, and rheumatism will have its way. Being unable to stand, his portrait was first taken by Mr. Andrew when sitting, and afterwards in the conveyance in which he travels over his dominions—a kind of hand-barrow made of rough tree-stems very roughly put together. For the rest, Jibberik speaks English in his own way, is powerfully built, and must have been an active man with plenty of brains and energy. He is anxious, like all the natives, to "belong Peritanè,"—but a greater than Jibberik has put an annexing hand upon him, and German he is now bound to be.

Alas for Leilikè, the young and the brave! He, with 200 others, went from Majuro to Auha, an island about 100 miles to the north. His object was to help the people there against an attack from neighbouring islanders. The party with him consisted chiefly of Auha men, who had been to Majuro on a visit. They left about a year ago and have not since been heard of, but the remains of some of their canoes were picked up on the reef at Milli.

Remi—old Remi, as he is fondly called—is Jibberik's elder brother, and the rightful monarch if he chose to assert his claim. But he willingly gave way, being a mild, kindly man without any ambition to rule. His heart was wrapped up in a crippled son who lately died, and for whom his affection was so strong that he had a house put up over the grave and has continued to sleep in it ever since. Remi is a great favourite with all Europeans, and it did not take long to make me share the feeling.

Far different to Jibberik was the King of Nukunono, the only Catholic king whom we met in the thousands of miles over which we travelled. We found this potentate a veritable King Cole, a merry old soul, playing a rude native drum with great skill, singing to his own accompaniment, full of life and action, and with a queen as fat and as merry and goodhearted as himself. His subjects are few, not over 100 in the whole island. They do not regard him with the awe that Jibberik inspires, but they love and obey him, and appeared to be a bright and happy people. Long life to him, and to old King John of Atafu, and to numerous other good and honest potentates in these far away lagoon islands. May they yet achieve their great desire and "belong Peritanè," instead of being forced under the flag of other nations.

At Nukunono, by the way, I witnessed another occurrence that struck me as remarkable. The Catholic native missionary, a fine-looking elderly man not distinguishable in dress and manner from the rest of his people, was actually assisting them, by words of encouragement and an occasional helping hand, to ship the copra from the beach to our vessel. He may have been an exceptional case, but the traders say it is not so and that native missionaries trained at the Church of England and Roman Catholic schools, generally turn out alike in this respect. We did not fall in with other Catholic missions and those of the Church of England were quite out of our way, so I cannot speak from any further observation of my own.

At Arurai there was no king, and many other islands are in the same position, divided into tribes each with its own chief. Sometimes the tribes quarrel with each other, but as a rule they make copra and live in peace together. At Ahrno, for example, the young and handsome chief, Uijelan, instead of counting the skulls of his enemies was counting cocoanuts which he had just sold to the trader. They were put into piles of twenty each, and a stone for each five piles enabled him to count by hundreds. Uijelan was shown some photographs, and became very anxious to have his own taken. This was promised if he would put on his native dress instead of the absurd women's cotton gown which it is the fashion for these men to wear. No chief was at hand to lend him a proper dress, and so rigid is caste in these little out-of-the-way islets, that he abandoned the portrait rather than put on, even for a moment, the very fine native dress which old Charley Douglas borrowed from another man, who was, unfortunately, only a common person. This leads me to mention a curious natural law which I noted among these natives. Properly formulated, the law would read, that the more ignorant the people the sharper, more defined and more rigidly maintained were their caste distinctions.

No notice of the sovereigns of these lagoon islands would be complete if it omitted the most important of all, Tem-Bainooke of Apemana, son and successor of the Tem-Baiteke whose slaughter of the white residents in his dominions has been already mentioned. Tem-Bainooke's sovereignty extends over three fine lagoons, Apemana, Aramuka, and Kuria, very fertile in cocoanuts, and with a population of 6000 to 7000 souls. Two of these are lagoon islands and the third is a raised coral island. They are part of the Kingsmill group, and it was with great regret we had to pass Apemana without calling. We had fallen to leeward, and the strong current in that part of the ocean would have caused too much delay; but I was able to get the most trustworthy accounts of this comparatively great king. Tem-Bainooke is a very large and a very fat man, so large and fat that when he boards a vessel he brings his own side ladder with him. He is absolute and does what he likes with his people. What he most likes is sending them away to work on colonial plantations and pocketing their wages when they return. Of course once away they need not return unless they liked, but as a rule they do return, and feel it a great honour that they should be able thus to help their king and have the light of his countenance shining upon them. Some meaner spirits have preferred keeping their wages. Their lot is a hard one, for their friends and their native land must see them no more. A short shrift—in fact no shrift at all—would be their fate at the hands of an outraged and defrauded king, by whose gracious favour they were permitted to live to an age at which they could earn money at all. A word from him would have caused their death at any moment. He had not said that word, and yet they were ungrateful. Such, however, is human nature, even in a coral island.

I should like to have heard Tem-Bainooke's opinions on these and other interesting points, and to have seen his house which, by all accounts, must be *unique*. Built on high wooden posts it forms two stories. In the lower he keeps his wives who vary in number from time to time but average three and twenty. The house is large and as the ladies, even in royal families on those islands, are content with a mat on the floor, there is no doubt ample room for many more. Tem-Bainooke's mode of dealing with his wives in ordinary matters is very summary, not to say startling. One among the number being ill, the master of a trading-ship who had somehow gained a medical reputation, was consulted by Tem-Bainooke about her. He pronounced the poor woman incurable. "Think me better shoot him" (meaning "her"), was the Sovereign's prompt reply. The doctor was horror-struck, and at once modified his opinion; and the poor woman's life was, for the moment at all events, spared. Not that I believe she would have much minded being killed. It was her lord and master's will and she would probably have cheerfully submitted, for they bring up women in Apemana without any nonsense about women's rights—especially when kings are concerned in the matter.

Over the harem is a second floor filled with costly incongruities—musical boxes, pistols, rifles, watches, clocks, lamps, highly-coloured pictures, pencil-cases, photographic albums (with musical boxes inside), and all kinds of showy rubbish—to which he had taken a fancy when opportunity offered. In the centre of the room stands a large earthenware bowl of water, holding bottles of wine and of water to be cooled for his own and his guests' drinking. Under the verandah are shelves well stored with supplies of tinned meats and other European food, as well as with wines, spirits, and beer.

Tem-Bainooke has not allowed any white man to settle in his dominions since his father so effectually freed himself of those who made the attempt in former years. Not even a missionary must settle there. He does all his own business. He sells his own copra, and also that of his subjects when money is scarce or when he fancies a new boat or any other expensive commodity. Tem-Bainooke, however, is human, and made a mistake two or three years ago in attacking Nanouts, a neighbouring island whose people he brought as prisoners to Apemana. H.M.S. *Dart* was sent to look into the case, and her commander, after full inquiry, sent back the captives to their homes. To avoid further trouble he also insisted on the surrender of the fine store of firearms that Tem-Bainooke had gathered, and sunk them fathoms deep in the lagoon.

When I add that this great fat creature has five of his women told off daily to wait upon him, and that one of their chief duties is to puff tobacco-smoke from their pipes into his royal mouth in order to save him the labour of smoking, it will be admitted that I have a right to feel aggrieved at the equatorial current which cruelly swept our vessel past Tem-Bainooke's shores, and prevented my having a personal interview with so interesting a Sovereign. Despite the *Dart's* doings, the release of his captives and the loss of his arsenals, King Tem-Bainooke adopts the English dress, tries to follow English manners and customs; and would be quite ready to " belong Peritane" to-morrow, if he thought any other country likely to annex him.

Turning from Apemana to another community even more remarkable, let me speak of our visit to Pleasant Island, so named by the master of the whaling-ship by whom it was discovered. The island may have deserved the name then but certainly does not now. A raised coral island without good harbour or anchorage and not more than sixteen or eighteen miles in circumference, it stands alone in the ocean, 150 miles from any other land, a few miles south of the Equator and within the territory which England has agreed to leave to German control. Pleasant Island does not much exceed 100 feet in height at any part. In the centre may be seen the remains of the old lagoon, reduced to a small depression swampy in some parts but, like the rest of the country, covered with trees, chiefly cocoanut-palms. The island used to be very productive in copra. The yield has fallen off materially and so have the people, through the sanguinary tribal feuds which have of late years distracted this little world. The population does not now exceed a thousand souls. There are ten white traders, some representing Auckland and German firms, others on their own account, and all of them settled at short distances from each other round the coast.

Landing on the reef, the vessel meanwhile beating about in the offing, we were welcomed by several of the traders assembled to receive us. Going with them to Henderson and Macfarlane's store, close at hand, a small crowd of natives soon surrounded us. They were in high good humour, but all the men and most of the boys were armed with repeating-rifles and carbines. The dress of both sexes consisted only of a short kilt of pandanus leaves hanging to a string round the waist, and each of the armed crowd had slung over his shoulder a pouch well supplied with ammunition. Despite their formidable get-up, the people had a kindly look with fine open eyes and magnificent teeth. Polynesians, one would say at a glance, but well dashed with Indian blood if the slight, active, and graceful forms of the women might be accepted as an indication.

One of the traders, Mr. Harris, had been on the island forty-five years, and was the oldest resident. He is seventy-four years of age,

A Pleasant Island Warrior.

hale and hearty, and looking, with his fresh-coloured face and heavy grey moustache, more like an old *militaire* than a Pacific Island trader. Mr. Harris kindly offered me a bed—a mat, to speak more correctly—in his house about half a mile further along the coast, and I anticipated a long and pleasant chat with the old man about the affairs and past history of Pleasant Island. Before starting for the house, it came out incidentally that his son, a lad of sixteen, had been shot in a fight and was lying dead in a small room put up for the purpose. He had been lying there some time—since the 29th December, in fact, and this was the 22nd January. I felt a natural delicacy in asking at what distance from his house the room had been put up. But calling to mind that Mr. Blowè, another trader, had also offered me his hospitality, I made excuse to Mr. Harris on the score of his terrible family bereavement. The old gentleman said, " Yes, it was terrible. It was the second son he had lost in the same way. This one would not rest till he had a chance of revenging his brother. He had gone out with some other lads in the same position, and this was the result. He had done his best to keep the lad without a gun, but the rest of them jeered him, called him girl, and made the boy so miserable that at last he had to give way. If he had only known what the boy was after, he should never have had the gun; but there was the trouble. His mind was bent on fighting, and he would have managed to get hold of a gun somehow. As to burying the body, the mother and the sisters would not hear of it. They were natives, and had a strong feeling against putting those they loved underground. In time they buried the bones, just like the New Zealand Maoris, and in the meanwhile they burned scented gums and put leaves on the body, and were crying over the poor boy continually. It was very sad, so different to what the island used to be when he came to it; and if something wasn't done soon, he didn't see what was to be the end of it all." Arranging with Mr. Harris to call on him next morning, I started with Mr. Blowè for his place about a mile and a half in the opposite direction.

Going along, Mr. Blowè suggested, as it was getting dusk, that it might be as well to walk along the beach instead of taking the path on the top of the low ridge. "Not that there is any fear," he added, "of the natives firing at us, but in the dusk they might mistake us for their countrymen, or we might be in the line of fire without knowing. It was as well to be on the safe side"—a sentiment in which I readily concurred; and along the beach we went accordingly.

"Now," said Mr. Blowè, suddenly stopping after we had gone some distance, "I must show you the new style of fortification in this country." He stepped off the beach, and a few paces inland brought us to a small collection of native houses with their new fortification, which consisted of thin wires obtained by unstranding some galvanized iron rigging. The wires, cunningly crossed and recrossed, formed a maze of low network round the houses, spreading horizontally a foot or so from the ground.

"You see," said Mr. Blowè, "this is to trip up any fellows coming in the night to surprise and shoot them."

Happy, happy island, thought I; well called Pleasant. What a delightful place to live in, especially with a growing family!

At last we reached Mr. Blowè's—a well-built house standing on tall posts, with galvanized iron roof and in all respects a comfortable place enough. Mr. Blowè had been round the various islands with a German war-ship, and acted as interpreter on her visit of annexation. He understood the natives well, and I passed an agreeable evening; but at one time there was just a little jar. He was telling me that he had only been two months at Pleasant Island, and had bought the place and business from one Hanson, to whom it came from Jim Mitchell.

"Jim was shot, you know, by the natives, and was buried just underneath where you're sitting."

Involuntarily I moved the chair a foot or two further from the spot, but was relieved on hearing that this little incident had occurred more than three years ago. I was further relieved by finding that it was entirely Jim's fault.

"He was one of the old set, you know, who used to bully the natives when they had no guns, and he wanted to carry on this game to the last. But when the natives got guns, they kicked at this sort of thing, you know, and then there were rows. One day, after hard drinking, Jim went out, gun in hand, vowing vengeance against the first native he came near. They tried to shoot Jim instead, but he dodged behind a cocoanut-tree. The natives dodged too, and finally got the best of it. It was Jim's own fault—not the least doubt of it, you know." He would show me the cocoanut-tree to-morrow, which he did, and I came to the conclusion that it must have been close quarters considering what poor shots the natives are and the number of holes they had managed to make in the tree.

One more little surprise awaited me. Glancing up at the roof, I noticed certain ugly-looking marks there.

"Ah!" said Mr. Blowè; "those are bullet-holes, but they were done in Hanson's time. So was that other hole you see in the door, and the one in the partition; the same ball did both. But I think they must have been accidental, for the natives have no animosity against white men. At all events," he added, "I am quite satisfied, and barring accidents don't feel the least concern."

With which comforting reflection I turned in and, being tired, slept too soundly to hear the firing in the night that disturbed not only my host, Mr. Blowè, but woke up Mr. Dunnett and Mr. Andrew who were staying at the houses of other traders close to where the firing took place. The traders took no notice.

"They are always at it," they tell you; "blazing away at each other, but luckily not doing so much mischief as one would expect." Still, it was very bad, and caused a great falling off in copra, and it was high time a stop was put to the whole thing.

I was curious to learn the origin of all this strife and bloodshed. It arose from a trifling circumstance at a marriage feast about ten years ago. A great collection of bottles of cocoa-nut oil was made as a present for the bride. Others (for the bridesmaids, I presume) were hung round the walls of the building in which the people were assembled. They were happy and agreed together in those days at Pleasant Island. The young men were joking over these bottles of oil, and one young chief in a bit of a temper prohibited another from meddling with a particular bottle on some ground of native etiquette. A quarrel ensued. They had been drinking "that hellish sour toddy," as Mr. Harris called it, and an old horse-pistol, unfortunately handy, was fired. In the *mêlée* the wrong man was shot, a young chief of great connections and of high family.

The feud thus begun has extended widely

since. Certain natives, no great number, living in the centre of the island and having their relations on the coast, make a practice of coming down to join their coast friends in shooting their enemies. Almost every village along the little coast has thus become involved and is at deadly feud with its neighbour. The fighting is in itself an absurdity, in fact not fighting at all. Small parties skulk about and blaze away at other parties at long distances on speculation, but shoot remorselessly any unfortunate man, woman, or child of the enemy's tribe who may chance to fall in the way of these "braves" or "warriors," as they call themselves. The whole crowd might be disarmed in less than a week by twenty or thirty sailors with native scouts to guide them, and I sincerely hope the German authorities will take the work in hand, as they only have the power to do so. As to the natives, it seemed to me they have had enough of it and would be very glad to be disarmed if it were done to all simultaneously. The position in this respect is easily understood, especially when we consider how many great nations in Europe are at the present time in much the same quandary, and would be glad to disarm " if only," as the Pleasant Islanders say, "the other fellow will begin." It is "that other fellow" who is doing all the mischief at Pleasant Island as elsewhere. He always does.

Mr. Harris gave me many interesting details about the island as it used to be when he kept as many as 500 hogs in his fences to sell to the whalers in the days when whale oil was supreme. About fifteen years ago some Kingsmill natives went to Ocean Island and taught the people there to make "sour toddy," by fermenting the sweet liquid which drops freely from the severed green fruit shoot of the cocoanut tree. Seeing the mischief, the chiefs of Ocean Island made short work of the matter. They gave the Kingsmill visitors their choice, to leave in certain canoes which were presented to them and take their chance of landing elsewhere, or to remain behind and be killed. The visitors took the canoes and unhappily reached Pleasant Island safely; and that, said Mr. Harris, is how the "hellish toddy" came here. Till then every village had its big house in which the people used to dance and sing. Now they dare not even go to the beach to ship a few bags of copra without taking their arms to guard against surprise. I handled a good many of the rifles, which the natives allowed me to do readily. They were in capital order, small bores of good quality and expensive pieces. The bores were not uniform, and the supply of ammunition must be considerable to keep them all going. The kinds I noticed were the Mauser, Winchester, Remington, Kennedy, Express, Spencer, and Martini-Henry. Gevelots were also there, and even one of Evan's thirty-four repeaters, so that the variety was as great as it well could be.

Mr. Harris had a strong desire to leave the place where he has so long lived. He wished to take passage with us to Strong's Island (Kusaie), the head-quarters of the American Mission, and to get the remainder of his children taught at the mission school. We could not take him, as no one is allowed to settle in Kusaie without permission. I promised however to state his case, and had much pleasure in writing to Kusaie from Ponapè. He offered, if allowed to settle at Kusaie, to give his house and ground at Pleasant Island for a mission station. I cannot tell what the mission authorities at Kusaie will see fit to do, but may express a hope that the old man will be successful in saving his young family from growing up amid such wretched ignorance and barbarism. It would be also pleasant to find his offer lead to the establishment of a mission and the restoration to peace and prosperity of this singular little island and its naturally pleasant people.

CHAPTER VII.

MISSIONARY WORK IN THE PACIFIC.

Rigid observances—Missionaries and the Areois—Results of the conflict—Meaning of conversion—A transition state—Absence of amusement—Want of mental occupation—Mischievous prohibitions—The Turi and its ways at Manihiki—The stocks—Feud of missionary and trader—Connubial relations—Teaching English—The Rev. Robert Logan—His station at Ruk—Missionary labours at Lukunor—Weaving at Lukunor—Churches in the Western Pacific—Churches in the East—Roman Catholic Church—Respective spheres of operation—Characteristic difficulties—Hard laws and a trader's opinion—Necessity for healthy pastimes—A new departure imperative.

No one can read of missionary work in the Pacific without admiration for the men who abandoned home and friends to go to unknown and savage lands in the service of their Master. But only they who have witnessed the result of their labours can fully appreciate the work that has been done. Landing among cannibals of whose language and customs they were ignorant, their own lives and the lives of their families in frequent peril, and deprived of all congenial society, the missionaries fought for years a weary and disheartening battle. A marvellous success ultimately crowned their labour and from end to end of the broad Pacific heathenism, in its old repulsive form, is now a thing of the past. Christianity is professed in the greater number of the islands, and before many years the remainder will be brought under its beneficent influence.

Reading attentively the missionary records, picturing to myself the heroic men and women among the founders of the work and witnessing the results that have been achieved, I feel that it is becoming in any one who ventures to take the part of critic to do so in a spirit of reverence due to the subject and the men. In such spirit, and in no cavilling vein, I desire to approach the question and to state my deep conviction, shared by many of the missionaries themselves, that a new departure has become imperative if further progress is to be made or that of the past to be maintained. The missionary has broken down the old heathenism, and to him we must look for the new civilization to rise upon its ruins. If he fails, to whom can we turn and what hope can there be for the natives for whom such great sacrifices have been made?

The pregnant fact forces itself into prominence, that in many of the islands and Atolls where Christianity is most loudly professed and its observances are most rigidly enforced, there is still a dangerous void. The old amusements and dances were sternly repressed in the early days as relics of heathenism; but no healthy recreation was given in their place. The minds of the people are a perfect blank. They have no literature, no books, nothing to move the intellect or to please the taste, nothing on which a healthy progress can be based. They need instruction in useful handicrafts. They need a healthy public opinion to replace the rigid laws and system of *espionage* which now exist. Above all, they need the creation of a healthy family life in place of the communism which tinges every action, colours every thought, and exercises so baneful an influence over their lives. A great work truly, but a work which ought not to be impossible to those who have achieved so much. Only, for the new work a new order of men will probably be required.

The first missionaries, in 1798, found the

natives in the lowest condition of heathenism, and with heathenism in all its forms they would have no compromise. Take the society of the "Areois" of Tahiti as an illustration. One old missionary writer describes them as "legion-fiends of the voluptuous haunts of Belial," and so, to the old missionaries, they might well have appeared. They claimed a heavenly origin, tracing their descent from two brothers of Oro, the God of War. Celibacy was not enforced, but only a limited number were allowed to marry and no children were suffered to live. We are told that the Areois consisted generally of the cleverest and handsomest persons of both sexes and that they travelled from island to island in companies more or less numerous. They were bards and seers, danced and sang, and gave theatrical performances in which the priests and public personages were unsparingly ridiculed. In this way they treated passing events and their visits were looked forward to with delight. Divided into many classes or orders, each had its peculiar part to play, and each was regarded by the people with a different feeling. As a whole, this secret society inspired a strange mixture of reverence and fear, based probably on the belief in its divine origin and the mysterious rites by which alone admission could be gained to its ranks.

With these Areois the missionary waged relentless war. One of the first deacons of the Congregational Church at Huahine (in the Society Islands) was a reclaimed Areoi who became an earnest missionary to spread the new and better faith among his people. To the contest with this society, and to the indecency which generally marks heathen dances, much of the present system of rigid prohibition is probably due. Unfortunately when the natives were induced to break so thoroughly with the past, no sufficient effort was made to provide other and better amusements for the future. The Bible was translated, and it would be impossible to over-rate its value as a resource. The grandest of books, a whole library of religious thought, of history and poetry, and of narratives the most touching, the Bible has so far served for mental food and recreation. For music and song they had the hymn-book, of which they still make constant use. Will the Bible and the hymn-book alone suffice ? If they do not, what will become of these natives when the inevitable reaction sets in ?

It is necessary to understand what the conversion of natives really means if we would fairly grapple with this question. Occasionally there are bright exceptions, men of a high order and of high aspirations whose souls are stirred by the doctrines and teaching of the new religion. Such men are rare, and conversion is generally by order of the chief who is himself too often moved by the old, old feeling, that it is best to have the strongest God upon one's side. That the God of the white man must be stronger and greater and wiser than their own, was clear to the natives when they saw how great and strong and wise the white man had become. The old writers give many illustrations, "It is my wish," said one of the Samoan chiefs, "that the Christian religion should become universal among us. I look at the wisdom of these worshippers of Jehovah and see how superior they are to us in every respect. Their ships are like floating houses, so that they can traverse the tempest-driven ocean for months with safety, whereas if a breeze blow upon our canoes, they are in an instant upset and we thrown into the sea. Their persons are covered from head to foot in beautiful clothes, while we have nothing but a girdle of leaves. The God who has given his white worshippers these great things, must be wiser than our gods, for they have not given the like to us. We want all these articles, and my proposition is that the God who gave them should be our God." I take this extract from a work on Polynesia, published in 1842, by the Rev. Dr. Russell, of St. John's College, Oxford. The same excellent history gives a curious story of another of the great chiefs holding a family council, and deciding that either he or his family must become "missionary" as the natives still phrase conversion. He was not particular as to who should change, but thought it wise to have both gods on their side.

We have similar illustrations in the early records of all nations. A few higher minds grasp the great truths and appreciate the loftier thoughts in the new religion, but its influence on the mass depends upon the slow growth of custom, and time alone can engraft it upon their nature.

The transition state is that in which the natives are now living. All was once fresh and new, but the freshness is wearing off and the newness is gone. In what condition will they soon be left? Of course many things plain to us now were not understood, or were very faintly understood by the early missionaries. They would otherwise have probably been content to break less completely with the past, and have taken more pains to discriminate between pastimes that had a heathen significance and others of a more harmless kind. The earlier missionary churches did not make this distinction, and the provision of proper recreation for the natives is fast becoming a question of grave import, second only I venture to think to the provision of means for opening and improving their minds.

Playing cards are so strictly prohibited that I am almost afraid to say a word in their favour. Yet I know the great resource which they, with dominoes and draughts, have proved among the Maoris. I know, too, that but for our rubber on board the *Buster* (we were just four) the evenings would often have been dull, and probably we might not have pulled together so pleasantly as we did during a long seven months at sea. But music surely ought to be encouraged. At Christmas Island there are no inhabitants beyond the few taken there from time to time for the pearl fishery. When we visited Christmas Island there were only twelve people upon it in charge of a European. The men were Penrhyn natives. There were two women of that island, one being the European's wife, the other, her sister, on a visit. Panè (Fanny), the trader's wife, had an accordion, and managed some well-known simple tunes very well. I recognized "Home, Sweet Home," and "Auld Lang Syne," which she had picked up on the rare occasions when a man-of-war or other vessel visited Christmas Island. At Manihiki, and at most of the other islands in which a native missionary is settled, poor Panè would be heavily fined and her accordion confiscated, even as befell the harmless Jews' harps which vicious traders sought to introduce among the Manihiki people. The Turimen would execute the law, but they are only the puppets and the native missionary pulls the wires. Traders are particularly jealous of interference by the the Turi with their native wives. They resist it whenever possible, and maintain their right to freedom in these matters. How much better would it be to remove the restrictions from all, and to encourage the love of music where it is capable of giving so much innocent delight.

The Penrhyn natives at Christmas Island— all of them relations to the two women—were rigid in their Sabbath observance, and every weekday engaged in prayer, at frequent intervals, and sang their proper hymns. When natives leave their own island to work at others, one of the number is appointed to take mission charge of the party and is always vigilant in seeing that these exercises are properly performed. At Suwarrow we found a party of seven from Manihiki, in charge also of a European with a Manihiki wife. He was an old French sailor who had served in the French brigade in Mexico, had seen service in many parts of the world, and had lived for many years at Tahiti. This little band of natives had no music, but they sounded their native Lali and had their five services as regularly on Sunday and their hymns and other services as continuously on other days, as if still under the eye of their native missionary at Manihiki. The Sabbath was observed with peculiar rigidity. They kindled no fires and smoked no tobacco, attended church services, and spent the rest of the day listlessly lolling upon their mats or sleeping. Can this last? Can human nature stand it? And what form will the revolt and the reaction take? The natives have been converted more than twenty years, and this system has lasted during all that time. Now they move about more freely and are not likely to rest satisfied when they see affairs so differently managed in the lands from which their great teachers and lawgivers come.

In that wonderful microcosm, Manihiki—one of the loveliest lagoons with one of the pleasantest and brightest people—the bow, if I judged aright, is already strung to breaking point. On the charts the island is called Humphrey's, and has never, I believe, been visited by a man-of-war. The landing is not difficult. There is no anchorage but it is easy and safe for a vessel to stand off and on. I spent one night on shore and was hospitably provided with a bed in the house of the native missionary. It was Saturday night and he was hard at work writing his sermon for next day, evidently a conscientious man doing his best according to the light that was in him. My friend, Mr. Dunnett, took me to the Turi House (Parliament Buildings), a long building in which the Turimen were assembled, waiting the return of the herald who had gone to beat the curfew drum. On a rough bench in one corner lay King Aporo, to whom I had been introduced in the morning. Mr. Dunnett told them I was a Turiman from New Zealand, and my reception was markedly kind. I watched the herald as he came through the little village, loudly beating the drum and shouting at the highest pitch of his voice, "Aue rake. Aere Po. Tapu te Po" (Hear ye all. This is the night. It is sacred to sleep). At this cry the good people must extinguish all lights and go properly to bed. Any Turiman having a suspicious mind or moved by undue zeal, may steal quietly into a house and see for himself that all is well. Or he may perform any other of the vagaries to which I have before referred as usual among them. It was amusing to watch the herald as he entered the Turi house with an official strut not to be surpassed, even in an English crown colony, deposited his rude drum, and made his report in due form. The dim lights—ordinary tin oil lamps—were extinguished, and we too went off to our beds.

Next day I again visited the Turi house. Over the beams and in all the corners were strings of cocoanuts, the fines accumulated during the past week to be divided, according to custom, among the Turimen on Monday. Attached to one of the house posts was a double iron shackle, with a hinge at the lower end and a hasp and padlock at the upper. In this shackle the feet of prisoners are locked, to hold them in durance till tried. Outside I saw

the stocks, in which men and women are
pilloried when the enormity of their sins or
non-payment of fines calls for extra punishment. The stocks were formed of two heavy
logs of wood—the upper being movable—with
corresponding holes cut in each. The culprit
sits on the ground with his feet passed through
the holes. And if by chance men or women, or
both, are put into these stocks on Saturday
night, they must remain till Monday, as no
Turiman would dream of taking up a case on
Sunday. Luckily the climate is a mild one, as
it need be.

I have known among our Maori native missionaries some excellent men, and in Fiji have
met with similar examples. But as a rule—
a rule to which there are very few exceptions—
the native missionaries are not either by training, tradition, or habit, fitted to exercise the
power wielded by them in these little isolated
islands. Too often they are narrow, bigoted
and uninformed, and yet upon them the future
of this curious atoll world must very largely
depend. I must again then lay stress on
the importance of these teachers being properly trained, that they should be taught
some useful handicraft, taught English to give

them access to English books and newspapers, music in its simplest form, and generally be fitted to become wiser leaders and better guides for their people. It may be sometimes impossible to find the requisite combination of qualities in one man; but it ought to be easy to find a suitable colleague and as easy, in many of the islands, to find a trader who would gladly give his aid. But here comes in the chronic feud between missionary and trader to which I have already referred—a feud equally mischievous to both. I admit the difficulty, and that the trader often takes to wife one to whom he is only married after the old native fashion; but as a matter of fact, the woman is a wife according to native custom and thought. She does not in the least lose caste but rather the reverse, and if the trader leaves she will wait what they consider a decent period—three or even six months—for his return. Then, with the sanction and approval of all her friends, she will marry a native or the trader's successor. Her children if she dies, are eagerly adopted by relations to whom they are a delight when young, and at no time a burden. These women, it must be remembered, are incapable of being wives in our sense of the term. There is none of the companionship, none of the higher feeling, none of the purity in their own social relations that makes wedlock holy. These never have been and never can be found so long as communism exists among them. To compel a European to take such a wife to his own country would only be to make both miserable, and to land them in the first divorce court that might be accessible.

To some extent this difficulty is recognized even where natives are duly married by the missionary. If the husband leaves the island, the wife may, after three years, marry again. Sometimes the marriage of white men with native women is performed by the Turimen instead of by the Missionary. In all cases, as far as careful inquiry enabled me to judge, the white men are faithful to their wives, in what form soever the contract may be made. The testimony was equally strong that the native wives are often as faithful to them, but this is far from invariable. These connubial relations are no doubt a stumbling-block in the missionary's way. I cannot venture a suggestion for its removal, but have a strong conviction that St. Paul would have found the way to cut this knot and to clear away this cloud, as he did so many others laden with doubt and difficulty in his day. Let us hope that the light may fall in time on those who have St. Paul's work to do, and who will need all his wisdom and charity in dealing with such vexed questions in the new isles of the sea.

At Atafu several natives spoke English fairly. I asked how they had learned. The reply was that a trader had taken much pains to teach them " to make me explain myself" as one of the natives, to my great surprise, put it to me. If this could be extended, if the people could be taught to read English and so gain access to English books, the problem of their civilization would be solved. With what delight they would read of Jack the Giant-Killer and Aladdin's wonderful Lamp, or roam over the fairy region so dear to childhood, and pave the way for better things hereafter. I am putting my head into the lion's mouth, I fear, but risk the displeasure of those who regard such reading as sinful and frivolous. The shock that would be given to their supporters keeps many of the best missionaries silent, but there are others less reticent. One respected missionary in New Zealand, even as I write, is at issue with his superior authorities because he encouraged the Maoris of his district in getting up horse-races. If the power rested with me, he should be made a bishop straightway—only, by the bye, he belongs to a church strongly anti-episcopal. His case was perfectly clear. The Maoris are mad for racing, and surely it is better that their sports be carried on at home under the eye of a venerated pastor, than that they should fall into the hands of a drinking, gambling class, to learn evil and be fleeced to the last farthing.

At Lukunor, in the Carolines, we found at anchor the American mission-vessel *Morning Star*. It was Sunday and they sent us an invitation to attend the afternoon service. An American lady who had come in the vessel on a visit from Boston, played the harmonium, and we had a capital sermon from the Rev. Robert Logan. The *Morning Star* sailed next day, leaving Mr. Logan to visit the adjacent islands in native canoes, and to find his way back to his chief station Ruk, 120 miles distant, in a small half-decked boat of six or seven tons. I had the pleasure of frequently meeting Mr. Logan, as we stayed a few days painting the vessel in the Lukunor lagoon. Traders of all classes speak of him with great regard and respect. They told me that he was a Northerner who had fought through the American Civil War. The war ended, he became a missionary and had been formerly stationed at Ponape, but about two years ago was removed to Ruk. The islands at Ruk, or Hogoleu, are a large group of raised coral islands, enclosed by a reef 180 miles in circumference, and with a population of 12,000 to 15,000, notorious for their wild and daring piratical life. Hogoleu is one of the few places left in the atoll world which no trading-vessel ventures to visit unarmed, but Mr. Logan has lately taken up his station there with his wife and child. I gathered from him that he had made friends of the natives in his immediate neighbourhood and could entirely depend on them. Beyond that he could not say much, but he had faith. Patience, he added, was a necessary mission virtue. It was a monotonous life for a lady, but Mrs. Logan took a great interest in missionary work and was fond of her garden. He would have liked her to accompany him, but travelling so great a distance in canoes and small boats was neither safe nor agreeable. Conversing thus pleasantly with the tall, gaunt American, and looking into his kindly face and bright clear eye, the image of Abraham Lincoln rose involuntarily before me. I felt that here, too, was a man not likely to turn back from the work which he believed God had cast upon him, a man not only with force of character, but honest, sympathetic and fearless, and as anxious as any layman to find a solution for the difficulties that stand in the path of these people towards civilization. In such hands and to such men the solution might be safely left if they could be brought together, take common counsel, and decide upon a common course of action.

The prohibition against tobacco seems a needless addition to unavoidable stumbling-blocks, and tends to make Christianity burdensome to a people to whom smoking is the chief luxury. The disuse was rigidly insisted upon by the first American missionaries, and there might now, it is feared, be danger in any single missionary admitting the mistake. Nothing could show more clearly the need of great care in framing regulations to be enforced as religious observances. Curiously enough, while tobacco was prohibited, no attempt was made to make the natives abandon the dirty habit of smearing their bodies with turmeric and oil, or of twisting their hair into unseemly chignons on the top of the head. While we were at Lukunor, Mr. Logan succeeded in getting eleven of them to cut their long hair, and the innovation caused a considerable stir in the little community.

I should be glad to hear that it had been followed by their abandonment of the use of *taik*, as they call the mixture of turmeric and oil with which they anoint themselves. The turmeric, if such it be, is grown only at Ruk, and the preparation a monopoly enabling the people of Ruk to export the article to all the adjacent islands. The mixture adheres to everything that a native wears or touches and is generally used to dye the mats which they weave for their own clothing. I saw a woman at Satoan weaving one of these mats which are remarkable for their neatness and finish. Seated on the ground, with a broad belt fixed round her waist to keep the threads taut, she worked with speed and skill, throwing the shuttle deftly and after each throw tightening up the threads thoroughly with a smooth piece of hard wood. At Satoan the mats are made of a fine fibre prepared from the bark of a shrub growing in profusion on many of the islands. At Ruk they are made from the fibre of the banana—veritable Manilla hemp. This is the woven cloth of which the early Spanish voyagers speak, and on the existence of which doubt has been since cast by many writers who would find their doubts dispelled by a visit to Satoan. Two mats, sewn together at one end with a small opening left in the centre, form a Spanish poncho, the universal and only dress among the uncivilized natives. Dyed with the *taik*, the poncho is of a bright yellow, so bright that I should think the *taik* would be regarded as a valuable dye anywhere.

At Lukunor I managed to get a copy of the "Kapas Fel" or Bible Stories, which have been translated into the native tongue. Mr. Logan is said to be the translator, but the little book bears no name. It is illustrated with the good old pictures which happily are not yet superseded in the Carolines by ground-plans of the temple or photographs of Jerusalem. The great round world is floating in space on the eve of creation. Adam and Eve are in the glorious garden of Eden. The rainbow of promise, the Tower of Babel,

Hagar and Ishmael, Abraham offering up Isaac, Joseph sold into captivity, Samson carrying off the gates of Gaza, all the old well-remembered pictures are in the " Kapas Fel." The book has several maps and much descriptive matter, and must altogether be the most attractive and useful reading which the natives possess. Multiply such books, and who can tell the good they would do in exciting to activity these sluggish and childish minds.

The churches put up by the natives under the English mission in the Eastern islands are larger and of far higher finish than those in the West under their American brethren. Whether this be the result of greater poverty or of a well-considered policy, I cannot say. Some of the churches in the Eastern Pacific are very large and good. At Niuè they are solidly built of coral rock; one of them, at Alofi being 130 feet long by 30 feet broad. But Niuè is a larger island, and the comparison with an atoll would not apply.

At Manihiki there are two large well-finished churches, one in each village, while in other Eastern islands the churches are equally good. At Nui, a small island of which Kirisomè has been missionary for many years, there is a

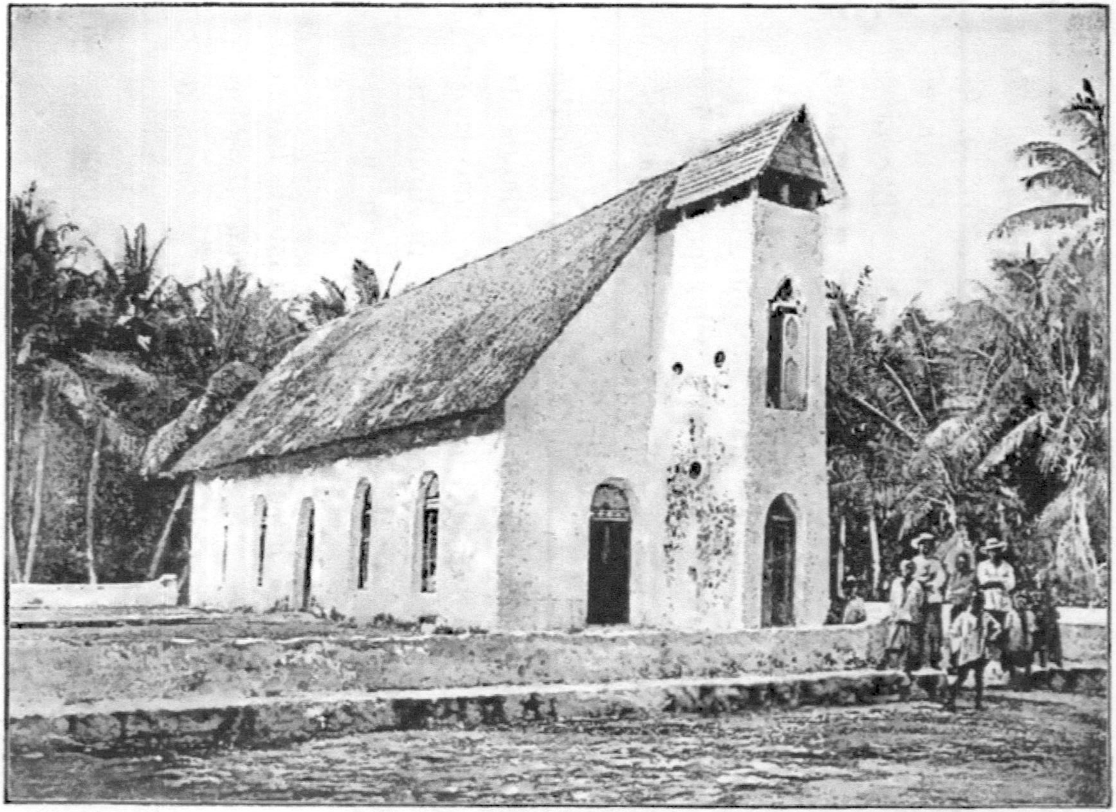

Copyright.

Photographed by Mr. Andrew.

Native Church, Manihiki.

very large stone church, 160 feet by 35; and at Atafu, with a similarly small population, a church of the same kind, 95 feet by 30. At Nukufetau I noticed that there was painted on the door "Siona, April 8, 1867," so that it could be little more than twenty years since Christianity was adopted in that island.

Entering one of these churches, the only furniture to be seen is the pulpit, with a space railed off on each side. One of these spaces is for the king's family, the other for the missionary's. The congregation sit on mats on the floor in their accustomed way, or on low, narrow benches fixed across the building. Occasionally there is very tasteful ornamentation by inlaid pearl-shell, or plaited cocoanut fibre dyed in many colours. The wood is also coloured, and sometimes ornamented with geometrical designs, but generally the interior is very plain.

The only Roman Catholic churches I saw were a small one at Fakaafu, and another of larger size at Nukunono. The interior of the latter is decorated with highly-coloured pictures. The crucifix is large and good, and the font an enormous Tridacna shell on a coral pedestal.

A smaller shell is built into the wall near the door for holy water. In front of the church stands a large wooden cross, and from a flag-staff at its side floats a white banner. From the letters on the banner I infer that the mission is Marist but the native teacher could not apparently say. The decorations of the altar were very curious and characteristic. There were a few candlesticks of brass, and several small jam tins covered with coloured paper and filled with pure white coral sand. A thin stick adorned with bits of different-coloured bright cloth, was placed in each tin and did duty for the flowers of which these poor islanders are so destitute. At this island the natives are all Catholic, as described in a former chapter.

At Fakaafu the people are nearly all Protestant, and the Catholics consist chiefly of the descendants of Portuguese from Samoa who have settled in Fakaafu. At Funafuti there is only one Catholic, an old man who, after spending some years as a visitor to his relations at Nukunono, went back to Funafuti to die among his own people. They had become staunch Protestants during his absence. Poor Elemia (Jeremiah) was a firm Catholic and his life became miserable, but he continued staunch for a long time. At last he gave way and attended the Protestant services; but, as he put it himself, "leg he go, belly (heart) he no go." Poor old Jeremiah, he stood out as long and as manfully as he could, but what was he to do alone among so many?

The mission work of the Pacific, so far as the Protestant churches are concerned, is so arranged that the one does not interfere with the other. The Church of England has its head-quarters at Norfolk Island and operates in Melanesia, that is to say, in the islands extending north of Norfolk Island to the equator, with the exception of a part of the New Hebrides which is under the care of the Presbyterian Mission from Victoria.

The Central and Eastern Pacific are Wesleyan and Congregational. The Wesleyans have the compact and populous islands of Fiji, the Friendly Islands and the small island of Rotumah, and have stations also at New Britain and other of the Western islands in that neighbourhood. The Congregationalists (English) have the Eastern islands extending from Tahiti to the Kingsmills, include all the Tahitian and Samoan groups, and have also taken in hand part of New Guinea. They are connected with the London Missionary Society.

Westward of the Kingsmills, all the islands north of the equator are taken in hand by the American Congregationalists connected with the Boston Board of Foreign Missions.

The Church of England educates its native teachers at Norfolk Island and sends some of them to complete their training in New Zealand. The English Congregationalists have their training school at Rarotonga (Hervey Group), and the Americans have theirs at Kusaie in the Carolines. The population in the Wesleyan districts is so concentrated and numerous that the white missionaries can be kept comparatively near each other and train native teachers on the spot. The Presbyterians train theirs under somewhat similar conditions at the New Hebrides.

The Roman Catholics make no terms with the other missions and are scattered over the Pacific from east to west and north to south, chiefly in the French colonies and Fiji. Their head-quarters are at Uvea (Wallis Island), where they have a fine cathedral, convent, and schools, and where they train their native teachers.

It will be readily understood that each of these churches has its own peculiar work and difficulties. The Church of England has carried Christianity into large groups and many islands, but they have still savages—Papuan savages—to be encountered and overcome. The Wesleyans, in their more compact district, have no difficulties of this kind now before them, but they have lately opened new ground among the savages of New Britain and other Western islands. In the East the English Congregationalists have banished heathenism, but they, too, have extended their operations to the barbarous New Guinea. Their American brethren have still much heathenism to contend with in their widely-scattered islands, but all of it is heathenism more or less tempered by intercourse with traders and with their own Christian fellow-countrymen. The Congregational missions of both countries have, however, much the greater share of the isolated atolls to which I have so often referred. The responsibility of providing properly-trained teachers for these atolls is exceptionally great, as I trust I have succeeded in showing in previous chapters.

The natives in most of the islands are in a

transition state, and rigid laws, appropriate perhaps in their day, do incalculable mischief now. "The harder they make the laws, the more they spy on the people the worse they make them," said a trader to me, and I thoroughly believe him. There is so much natural brightness, so much attractiveness in these people, that none can look without concern at the prospect before them. Are they to die of inanition and of the vices to which inanition gives birth? Left altogether to themselves, they might gradually have risen into civilization. To-day a poet might be born; to-morrow an historian or a law-giver. The people would rise by degrees and gradually adapt themselves to the new life, but that has become impossible. Civilization is being forced into them from without, not growing slowly from within. With the keenest appreciation of the great difficulties that have been overcome, I have yet a strong conviction that the old methods are worn out and that a new departure is inevitable. The weakness of the present system I have ventured already to indicate, and more than this I am not vain enough to attempt. A convocation of the missionary churches of all denominations might be held and the question be maturely considered by them. Then could we hope to see the dull, endless round of the present system disappear, and look forward to a brighter future for these islands and their inhabitants. It is imperative that more varied work should be found. There is ample room for improvement in the few crops they grow, in the pigs and poultry which they breed, in the manufacture of the tortoise shell and of the fibres and other material which they already, in many ways, so skilfully handle. They need more useful occupation, more healthy pastime and recreation mental and physical, wider instruction, a healthier public opinion, and a steady but cautious attack on their deadly communism.

To the various missions which have done so much in the past we must look for development in the future. Delay will be more than dangerous, for unless the remedy be quickly found the doom of the native race is sealed. Disease born of vice, is already doing its deadly work, and the practices of old heathen times are again in use to prevent increase of population. In a change of system lies the only hope. If the change be in the right direction, the work of the past will continue to bear fruit and the way be opened to a higher civilization. If not, the race will surely perish, and heroic men and more heroic women will have toiled, and suffered, and sacrificed themselves in vain.

CHAPTER VIII.

A VISIT TO PONAPÈ, ITS RUINS, AND ITS PEOPLE.

The products of Ponapè—On the road to China and Japan—Pagans and Christians—Ravages of small-pox—At Kusaie by the way—At Pingelap and Mokal—Pet pigs—Pet frigate birds—Spanish man-of-war—Mr. Kubarri's work—Start for the ruins—A trader's hospitality—The islets on the reef—Massive and mysterious ruins—Who were the builders?—Native migrations—A pleasure trip from Atafu—Islanders born rovers—Islets of Ponapè apparently coral—A rough passage—Native customs—Heathen and Christian at Kitè—Mr. Begg of Ponapè—His career and opinions—Captain Edward Rodd, a Pacific celebrity—His early experiences and present opinions—Good-bye to the veterans—Recent massacre of Spanish governor and forty-five soldiers at Ponapè.

Ponapè stands prominent among the very few mountainous islands which vary the monotony of innumerable atolls in the Outer Pacific. The massive ruins of Ponapè are its most remarkable feature, speaking in their weird loneliness of some dead and forgotten race. By whom and for what purpose they were built are questions to which no answer has yet been given. A careful inspection of the country, and comparison with similar ruins if such there be in other countries, will give the only prospect of solving the mystery.

The present inhabitants of Ponapè can tell nothing about the ruins and attribute them to the devil, a solution perfectly satisfactory to their minds. They are incapable of conceiving the construction of such works, and the people who built them must have been of a race much more numerous and greatly in advance of the two or three thousand natives now occupying this large island. Of these natives, the accompanying photographs of the chief of a neighbouring group (the Mortlocks) dressed in his woven poncho, and of a young woman from the same group with the mats and elaborate belt already described, will give a fair idea.

Ponapè (or Ascension Island) is the largest of the Semiavine group, lying between 6° 43" and 7° 6" north latitude and in 158° 30" east longitude, and forming part of the Caroline Archipelago. The small Semiavine group appears to be the remains of a large island of which the greater part is now far below the ocean. Only a number of volcanic islands of varying size are left, representing, let us suppose, the mountain tops of the ancient land. These are surrounded by a coral reef built on the sunken flanks of the ancient mountains, and therefore extending now from the shore far out to sea. Two fine little lagoon islands seven or eight miles from Ponapè, lie outside the reef, and represent, let us also suppose, the remains of small islands lying off the coast of the old land but now sunk deep within the lagoons formed by the coral reefs built upon their respective slopes. These lagoon islands are known as Ants and Parkins, corruptions of the native names Antema and Pequena. The islets on the reefs of these two lagoons are richly clothed with cocoanuts, and are much prized by the natives of Ponapè who run down to them in their canoes, make large quantities of copra, and bring back supplies of nuts which their own mountainous volcanic island does not supply in the same perfection.

Ponapè Island stands in about the centre of the Semiavine group. Probably in far distant ages it was the summit of the great mountain range. To-day it is still broken and mountainous, about 60 miles in circumference, and attaining a height of 3000 feet. The shores and hill-sides are strewn with loose blocks of basalt, many of them perfect hexagonal prisms of considerable size. There are a few nice streams and there is some level land, but the peculiar stony character, as far as I could see or learn, applies to the greater portion of Ponapè. It is so marked as to suggest the idea that the whole island has been at one time terraced and cultivated, and that these rocks and prisms are the ruins of the terraces washed or fallen from the hills to the shore below. The scene spontaneously suggests this idea, so thickly strewn and numerous are the blocks, and so extensive is the area that they cover.

Between the rocks, and wherever they are cleared away, the soil is of great fertility. Bread fruit, vegetable ivory and cocoanut palms, and all tropical fruits flourish luxuriantly when planted, which they are not yet in any quantity. Very fine hardwood trees are abundant, and the houses, always on a raised foundation of loose rocks, are built and floored with huge roughly-hewn slabs of timber much like teak and mahogany.

From the stony shore the coral reef extends four or five miles out to sea. Generally this great reef is so level and the water so shallow, that boats can only get over it at half or high tide, but there are many breaks in the reef and some good harbours are thus formed. The usual larger channels also run parallel with the outer or ocean part of the reef and divide the whole into two distinct parts, known respectively as the outer or Ocean Reef and the inner or Shore Reef with the channel deep and blue between them. Ponapè lay formerly on the direct road from the West Coast of Spanish America to Manilla, and is said to have been a favourite resort of the Buccaneers. It is still in the road of sailing-vessels from Australia or New Zealand to China and Japan, and is much frequented by whalers from San Francisco. Five of these whalers (three being auxiliary steamers) were at anchor in Modoc Harbour on the opposite side of the island, and while we were at Kitè two of them passed us crowded with boats and men on their way to sea after getting supplies and water at Ponapè.

There are no towns, and of course no hotels. The natives live together in small numbers along the coast, and the interior of the country is quite uninhabited. The traders live also in detached houses along the coast, receiving produce brought to them by the natives, and selling to them in return. Travelling is entirely by boat or canoe, the mass of thickly-strewn boulders making land travel too difficult for ordinary purposes. The natives are divided into five tribes, of whom three have joined the American Mission established at the island. The other two are still heathens of the comparatively mild character that marks heathenism in these days. The Ponapè people are skilful workers, and Ponapè sleeping-mats are known over the whole Pacific. They are of peculiar make. Pandanus leaves are doubled and stitched together like thatch with one carefully-folded leaf sewn over the other so that they roll up easily, and are not only thick but soft and elastic.

The natives have abundance of turtle on their beaches, and pearl shell is found but not so worked as to yield any quantity. Tortoise shell is among their exports. The vegetable ivory nut is abundant, the sugar-cane very fine, and good coffee is produced but only on a small scale. The number of inhabitants does not exceed 2500, the small-pox having killed a great many about thirty years ago. A vessel came at that time into Modoc Harbour with the disease on board and landed her patients on Pariau a small island in the harbour. The captain warned the natives to keep off, and took supplies from them in his boats half way from the shore. But they managed to steal some sacks from the boats one day, and that was how the small-pox got into Ponapè. The houses are small and poor and only of one room, so that the disease must have proved a terrible scourge among the people.

The Ponapè canoes are very good, owing to the fine timber which enables the natives to use solid tree-trunks, instead of being obliged to build the hull with small planks fastened by twisted cocoanut fibre as in the atolls and other less favoured islands. As we enter the harbour of Jamestown, the first station established by the American Mission under the Rev. W. Doane is a prominent object in the view. The buildings are extensive and stand on a green-clad promontory, but are now in charge of a native teacher, as Mr. Doane is stationed at Metalaneum Harbour on the other side of the island, about twenty miles from Jamestown.

On the 26th January, 1887, we had sighted Kusaie (Strong's Island), the headquarters of the American Mission in the Western Pacific, but feared to land lest we should lose the chance of making the next island (Pingelap) before the following night. We determined, therefore, to pass on. I regretted this, not only because it lost me the opportunity of making the acquaintance of the American missionary, but because at Kusaie there are ruins smaller in extent but similar in character to those at Ponapè. We coasted along Kusaie, which is about thirty miles in circumference, with hills exceeding 2000 feet in height, with a very good harbour and a population of only 250 to 300 souls. We had a fine view of the mission buildings and schools at Kusaie, very prettily situated on the slopes of one of the hills. On the following day we reached Pingelap, landed there and sailed on to the next atoll, Mokal, which we reached just as the mission auxiliary steamer *Morning Star* was leaving. She had called to land Miss Fletcher, an American lady attached to the mission, who came to inspect the girls' school at Mokal and for whom the *Morning Star* was to call on her way back to Ponapè. I had not the pleasure of meeting Miss Fletcher who, after taking a much-needed rest, went at once

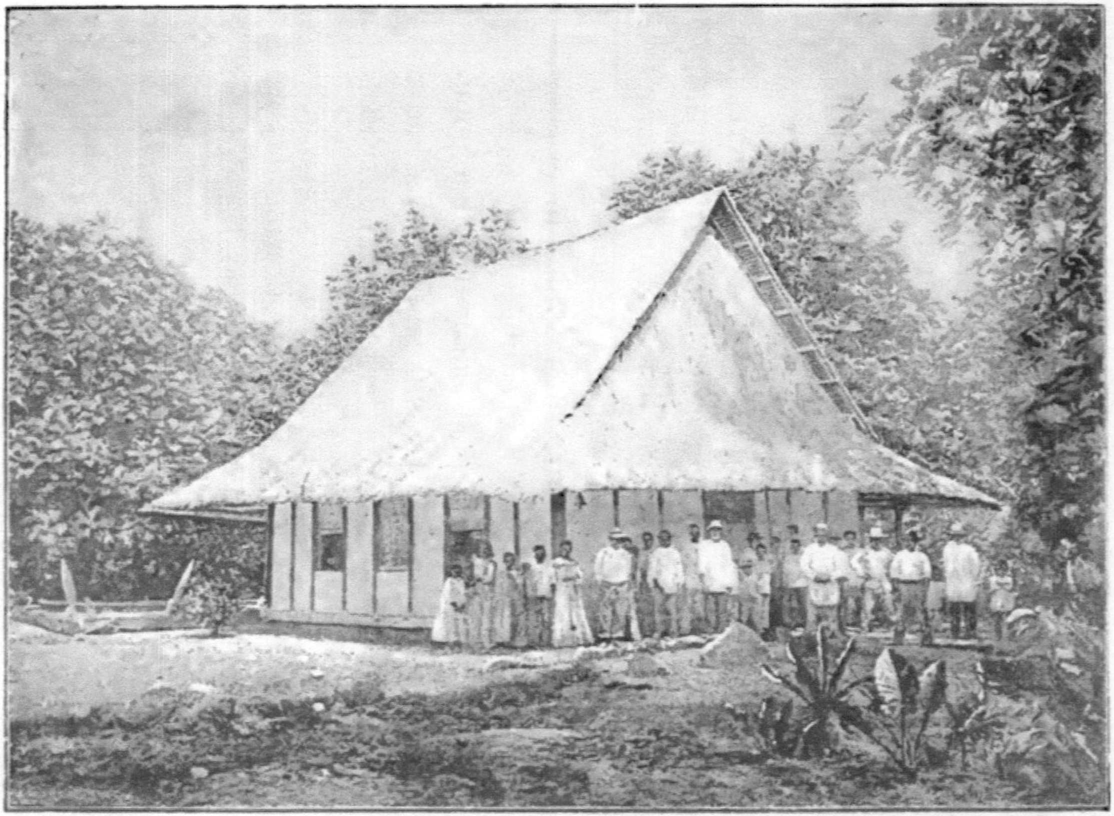

 Photographed by Mr. Andrew.

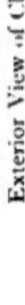

Exterior View of Church at Mokal.

to the native church service and my own stay was short at Mokal. The incident is worth mentioning, however, as an indication of the zeal and devotion for which missionary work calls. They only could sustain a lady amid the discomforts and the dearth of society which such visits necessarily entail.

At Pingelap, the land and the people are poor, but at Mokal both are richer. Pingelap has islets so narrow and low as to produce cocoanuts only, and in very moderate quantity. Mokal has islets much broader, and therefore with a greater variety of products. A Mokal native, in broken but very intelligible English, waxed eloquent in explaining the difference. He told me how the Pingelap people were so poor that they were glad to come over and work for the Mokal people under a two years' agreement, receiving at the end of the time a box filled with cotton prints and other articles.

"Is not that very little?" I asked.

"Oh, no," was the reply. "Pingelap man, he glad come." And then my informant added, "He rich man when he go Pingelap again."

This is the only case I met with of natives formally engaging themselves to other natives, or being formally hired by other natives as labourers.

The term labourers, be it at the same time understood, has not the meaning it would bear with us, for they are all related and live together, while copra-making is the most attractive of all employments to the native people.

I have referred to the great need for providing proper mental occupation and including healthy sports and pastimes in the course of mission training. The American Mission, except in its prohibition of tobacco, appears to be less rigid and to exact less conformity with European notions of dress than some of the other Congregational and Wesleyan Missions; but, even with their natives, a lamentable want of healthy mental recreation is apparent. I have frequently watched the heathens engaged in card-playing which they enjoy intensely. Surely the same taste might be turned to good account by introducing draughts and other harmless games. What would our own lives be without similar recreation, and wherein do these natives differ from ourselves? That they have an intense love of sport of all kinds is manifested in various ways. At Lukunor the small boys took the greatest delight in racing their little model canoes, just as our own youngsters do their model yachts. They spent hours in the sea

Girl of Mokal.

around our vessel, each lying at full length on a pointed log of wood or paddling himself upon it with hands and feet, and racing each other in this way from the ship, a quarter of a mile off, to the shore.

The fondness of the natives for birds and animals is also very marked, and would lead one to suppose it well worth taking the trouble to introduce better breeds on the islands. They have some wretched cats and some dogs of no describable kind at all. Their special pet is the pig; and it is astonishing to see the cleanliness of his habits and the knowingness of his look when thus allowed to mix on friendly terms with the family. He trots about with the children, follows them like a dog, gambols and plays with them, and acquires a habit of throwing his head on one side and looking up out of one eye with comical effect. At some islands they tame the "frigate," or "man-of-war" bird, which never fishes for itself, but circles in the air, watches till some other bird has picked up a fish; pounces upon the captor and robs him of his spoil. At Pleasant Island there are several structures of open framework built as roosts for these birds; and the chiefs vie with each other in possessing the greatest number. One of the birds is used as a decoy, and others are soon caught and tamed with him. They take their sea voyage daily in search of food and return to roost with the greatest regularity.

We left Mokal towards evening on the 28th, and early next morning sighted the high land of Ponapè, anchoring in the afternoon in the fine harbour of Jamestown on the north-west side of the island. The harbour was surveyed and named by the United States frigate *Jamestown*, and its original name is now never used. Native houses are to be seen, half hidden by trees, and a few traders' houses are scattered along the shore at considerable distances from each other. A beautiful little stream opens into the harbour, and the valley through which it runs, purchased from the natives by a Mr. Kubarri, is the only level land near. In front, around, and in all directions, are great hills of basalt and conical crater elevations. One of these hills is an excellent landmark resembling a huge sleeping dog. The head of the dog seemed to me a mass of distinct basaltic prisms like those that are strewn so thickly on the hill-sides and along the shore.

Ponapè, with the rest of the Carolines, has

View of Jamestown Harbour, Ponape.

been Spanish by discovery for the last three centuries, but no attempt until now has been made to interfere with it or its people. Roused by the German attempt at annexation, the Spaniards are moving at last and a Spanish war-ship from Manilla was at Ponapè for the first time in July, 1886. She hoisted the Spanish flag, and a proclamation was issued prohibiting the purchase of land. The captain promised to return in October, but had not done so up to the following January, the date of our visit.

The officers of the Spanish ship were very polite and considerate to the traders, giving them every assurance that they would be assisted in carrying on their business. The traders, therefore, look forward with great pleasure to the arrival of the Spanish governor and the opening of a Spanish mission. The Protestant missionaries do not share the pleasurable feeling. In no place does the unfortunate antagonism between missionary and trader seem stronger than at Ponapè. In no place could their co-operation be more beneficial to the natives who, in their natural state, are as low in ideas and as depraved in practice as they well could be.

The Spanish commander made a careful survey of the land round the harbour, with a view to selecting a site for a town. The only suitable site, with level land and fresh water and anchorage close up to the shore, is on the land owned by Mr. Kubarri (about 2500 acres), to which I have referred. It may be that the Spanish Government is negotiating for the land and that this is the cause of the delay in the ship's return. Mr. Kubarri was in Ponapè for three or four years as agent for Godeffroi and Co., and during his stay had made, I was told, a large collection of birds and plants, and taken many photographs. I have not been able, in New Zealand, to ascertain if he has published anything in connection with Ponapè and its ruins. He would probably have published in Hamburg, if at all.

The land near the harbour is soon exhausted for travelling purposes, it being hard work to get about on its rock-strewn shores. The stream I have referred to is the only place which one would care to visit a second time. We were anxious to start for the ruins, twenty-five miles down the coast on the other side of the island, but the weather was too wet and stormy to attempt the journey. At last a break occurred and we determined to run the risk. We had a good boat kindly lent by Mr. Rüss, agent of the German firm, who accompanied us on the trip. As boatmen we took one of our Penrhyn boys (Turoa), and one Caspar, a native of the little lagoon of Nukuor, who has lived some years at Ponapè. Both spoke tolerable English; but though coming from islands with so many hundreds of miles of ocean between and with people of so many other races intervening, Turoa and Caspar were evidently of the same original race and tongue and could understand each other perfectly.

Taking advantage of the break in the weather, we started on Tuesday morning with a pleasant breeze and began our long beat of fifteen miles to get round Takaihu Head near Metalaneum Harbour. After that the wind would be fair, so we hoped to get to the trader's house before light and tide should fail. Our course lay along the coast; sometimes in the wide deep channel between the ocean reef and the shore reef, and sometimes in channels with small islands on the one hand and Ponapè on the other. Often it was across long shallows impracticable for boats at low tide. In the afternoon the weather changed, and heavy rain and squalls made us thankful to stay for the night at Takaihu, which we reached at dusk. At Takaihu there is only the trader's small house, of the kind usual at Ponape. The owner received us most hospitably and we had a comfortable night's rest, none the less pleasant that the wind howling outside made the house delightfully cool, and effectually banished mosquitos.

At daylight, after a cup of excellent coffee and a breakfast of the renowned tinned meat of our own New Zealand, we started gaily and with every prospect of a splendid day. A run of a few miles, with a favourable wind, soon carried us into Metalaneum Harbour and past the Missionary Station which looked picturesque and homely among the fine trees on the beautiful hill-slope on which it stands. At nine o'clock we were running among a number of little low verdant islets, scattered for some miles over the shallow waters of the coral reef and distant about a mile from the high volcanic shore. The islets were thickly covered with trees, and, threading our way through them we came to a space, about 250 feet square, so regular that it looked at once as if formed by the hand of man. Channels, from 30 to 100 feet broad, debouched from this water-square like submerged streets or carefully

Ruins at Ponapé.
Photographed by Mr. Andrew.
Copyright.

made canals. We left the boat, and wading up one of the smaller channels over a soft mud bottom, were in a few minutes at the islet on which the ruins stand. Hidden by the overgrowing trees and vines till we were right in front, the ruins suddenly burst upon us, and amid the utter loneliness and dead quiet of the scene, were weird and startling in their unexpected grandeur and simplicity.

Before us rose a massive structure, 20 feet high and 170 feet broad, with walls of enormous thickness, formed of basaltic prisms, some of huge size, laid in alternate transverse rows the larger in one direction and the smaller in the other. It was the western wall on which we gazed in silent wonder, and through a great opening in the centre, evidently intended as an entrance, we could see the inner walls of the same height and character. The islet, like all through which we passed, was embanked with massive walls of the same style as the building. These careful embankments, the great walls, and the solemn silence, gave to the whole the appearance of a city dead and deserted now, but with canals once crowded by canoes filled with devotees eager to attend the savage rites and sacrifices of which the ruined mass before us may have been the sacred scene. That it was built for a temple seemed clear to my mind, and I think the reader, on hearing it described, will come to the same conclusion.

The weather began again to threaten, and no time was to be lost. Mr. Andrew proceeded to clear away as much of the luxuriant, overgrowing vines and shrubs as time allowed, and succeeded in taking some excellent photographs. Mr. Rüss and myself endeavoured to measure the walls and building. Our only means was by a rope, cut to what we judged five fathoms. With it we passed under the towering walls and pushed our way among the trees and shrubs as best we could in the short time at our command. Necessarily, therefore, the measurements are not exact, but with one exception they must be near the mark. That exception refers to the south and eastern walls, which bulged out in several places, overhung dangerously, and were thickly covered with shrubs, vines, and branches.

The building, according to our measurements, is 171 feet in the western front, with an open space of 15 feet in the centre for an entrance. The northern wall is 210 feet long, with a small low passage running through it, level

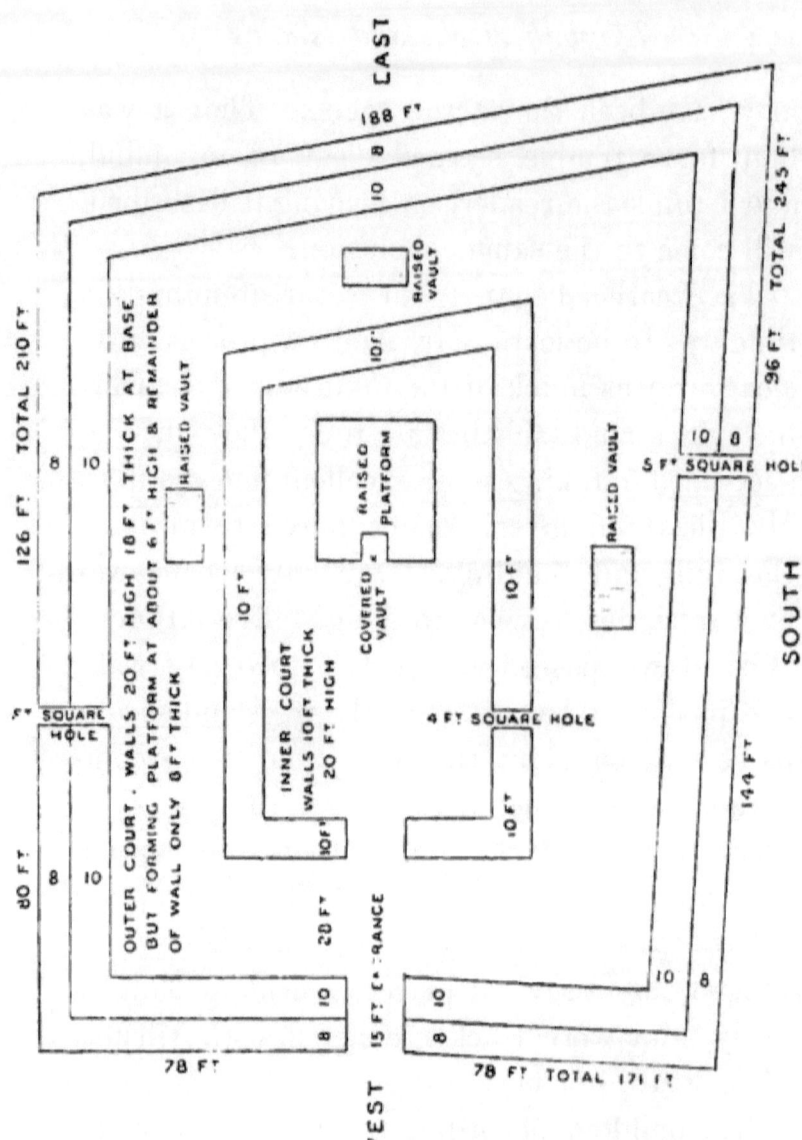

Ground Plan of Ruins at Ponapé.

with the ground and about four feet square. This hole or passage was distant 80 feet from the western end. The eastern wall is 210 feet long, and the southern 245, also with a hole or passage through it about five feet square, and distant 96 feet from the eastern end. The walls are 18 feet wide at the base, and continue of that width for the first six feet in height. For the remaining fourteen or fifteen feet they are reduced to eight feet in thickness, leaving a platform six feet from the ground and ten feet broad all round the inner side of the building.

About twenty-eight feet from the inner face of this wall there is another court with a similar opening opposite to the outer opening, and with one small low passage through the wall. The walls of this inner court are as high as the outer, but with a uniform thickness of only ten feet from base to summit. Near the east end of the inner court and fifty feet from its entrance, is a large raised platform, about forty feet square and six feet high, solidly built of the same prisms, and having in the centre of its front a vault five feet high and six feet broad. Three raised vaults of a similar structure and size are built in the outer court.

No sign of roof, door or window, or of preparation for either is to be seen. The platform, and the creek embankments, are as clearly useless for defence as these vaults would be for dungeons or buccaneer's treasure-chambers, as they have been respectively styled in old narratives. The opinion started on hearsay I fancy by Dumont D'Urville, that these buildings were put up by the buccaneers has been repeated in various works but will not stand investigation. No civilized people could have wasted time and labour in raising such a structure, but that some powerful savage chief should have conceived the idea of increasing his glory and perpetuating his name by a temple to his gods, and that his people should have eagerly abetted him, is quite intelligible. Far more inexplicable are the miles of careful embankment round the islets, forming into veritable canals the ocean-streamlets that meander through them. That the so-called vaults may have been designed for holding sacrifices, human or otherwise, and the passages through the walls intended to admit them, is also a reasonable surmise. One can even imagine them as receptacles for fuel, or in other ways connected with savage rites, but certainly not as hiding-places for a buccaneer's plunder.

Throughout the ruins the stones used are natural basaltic prisms. In no case are they squared or cut as old narratives say, and the embankments are of exactly the same structure.

A month spent among the islets by a party properly equipped to search for relics of the dead race that once inhabited them, might throw some light upon the origin of these mysterious ruins. A hasty visit of a few hours could end in little beyond roughly gathering the data that would convey a general idea of their character. The photograph and rough ground plan attached will, I hope, aid in making that idea more clear.

The photograph is taken at an angle with the entrance, and gives a sectional view of the wall at the base and the upper part of the embankment a few feet above the level of the creek. The rude character of the whole structure is apparent. Not a vestige of art or workmanship of any kind is to be seen. The most remarkable characteristic is the enormous size of some of the prisms. I measured one at the north-west corner of the wall, about seven feet from the ground. The length was thirteen feet and the breadth two and a half feet, and many others were of greater size and weight. The volcanic hills, apparent in every part of Ponapè, contain, no doubt, many columnar basaltic prisms. Their great length in proportion to width and depth, would make it more easy to convey them to the spot and raise them to a height, provided there were a sufficient number of men for the purpose.

Who, and of what race, were those men? Whence did they come, and whither have they vanished so effectually out of mind and memory as to leave not the slightest trace behind? The Rev. Mr. Ellis, Hermann Melville, and others have described vast structures (terraces and pyramids apparently) in Tahiti, in the Marquesas, and in other islands. Easter Island has numerous rude, gigantic statues of stone and wood, one of which has just been removed with great difficulty, and taken to America by the United States steamer *Mohican*. But the Ponapè ruins have a character peculiarly their own. Whence did the builders come, and whither have they gone? The latter question who can answer? The former is a more hopeful subject, and well worth investigation. I do not pretend to the knowledge necessary to form an opinion, but saw enough in the course of this voyage to suggest a belief that the Pacific

Islanders generally, are a very ancient people, more ancient than is usually thought. Their great migrations are described in the traditions of our New Zealand Maories, and many navigators have met modern proofs that the migratory spirit is still active among them. Accident often carries them much further to sea than they intended at starting; and Cook relates a striking illustration of this during his third voyage. Omai (Cook's interpreter) met on a far distant island three of his countrymen, " whose story," says Cook, " is an affecting one. About twenty persons had embarked in a canoe at Otaheite to cross over to the neighbouring island, Ulieta. They missed Ulieta, and passed many days without sustenance. Worn out by famine, only four survived, and of these one died soon after landing on the island to which the canoe drifted with them, and where they were kindly received and had settled definitely among the people."

At Penrhyn I met a native who, in 1883, started with five others in a boat for Manihiki, about 180 miles away. The trade-wind was with them. Others had done the trip in two days, and why not they? They missed the island somehow and were eight days at sea. "We would have died," he told me, "in another day but just found Manihiki in time." These Penrhyn people say that their own little island was first peopled by a Manihiki man (Mauta by name), who quarrelled with his own people and sailed off with a stolen canoe in high dudgeon. He found Penrhyn, and after a long absence returned to Manihiki, stole a couple of women, and sailed again to Penrhyn. A very old man (Toka Wharike) still goes from Manihiki at every chance offered by trading-vessels, to see his relations at Fanning's Island, 800 miles away. In his early days this man was a great traveller in his canoe. He went to Swain's Island, 600 miles distant, and returned to Manihiki safely. Again he went to Swain's Island, taking relations with him who settled on it and were finally bought out by Mr. Eli Jennings and taken back to Manihiki. Their love of travel is innate; they are born sailors, and have invaded and conquered in many directions. For example, at Nui, in the Ellice Group, we come suddenly on a people evidently of different race to that in the adjacent islands. Ask them, and they will tell you how, not very long ago apparently, their fathers came from

Taputeoua in the Kingsmills, conquered the original inhabitants and settled here. At Atafu only the year before last, nearly the whole population started on a pleasure trip to Nukunono and Fakaafu, distant fifty miles and 120 miles respectively. They tied six canoes in three pairs, and with these frail craft started gaily on their pleasure trip. After an absence of three weeks the pleasure party returned, but one shudders to think what might have been the fate of that gay crowd if wind had failed or the current had carried them away from their destination.

More pleasant was it to observe a large party that we took from Fakaafu to visit their friends at Atafu, carrying the finest of their young cocoanut plants and banana trees to improve the plantations of the friends they were going to see. It was a hopeful sign, and suggested the stimulus to progress that might be given if the missionary vessels made an effort in the same direction, not only with plants from other countries but with better breeds of birds and animals than the miserable kinds which the people now possess.

These islanders are born sailors and rovers. The sea is their home, and they ought to take a good position for tropical work in the future Australasian navies. The risk is that they will die out before the national aspirations in that direction are realized. On a few of the islands they build good boats, thanks to the gratuitous teaching of traders to which I have before referred; but in most of them the old canoe is still their only sea-going craft. The canoe is a very frail affair, always with an outrigger, and varying only in shape and size. Neither nails nor metal fastenings are used. The planks or bits of wood are fitted very neatly, and lashed together very tightly with cord made from the husk of the cocoanut. Some of the canoes, though narrow, are of considerable depth, and the outrigger enables them to carry very large sails of the leg of mutton shape. With these they sail very close to the wind but make great lee way. At Nakufetau I saw a perfect curiosity, a laborious imitation of a white man's boat, twenty-six feet long with five feet beam, and built entirely of pieces of wood lashed together. Of course the boat was a wretched affair, but did it not indicate a desire for improvement? It seemed to me a dumb but eloquent appeal for help in the direction I have ventured to indicate as that in which missionary work may find a new field for beneficent operation.

While gazing on the massive, mysterious ruins, and while the thoughts they suggest come rushing through the mind, we hear the rising moan of the wind, and the heavy rain clouds are gathering around. It is necessary we should get clear of these islets before the tide falls or we must spend the night among them. Very reluctantly, therefore, we left late in the afternoon, wading along the canals and drawing the boat after us, with new vistas of beauty opening at every turn. All the islets, as far as I could judge, were of coral formation; but on that point I feel by no means sure and it is one worth careful investigation. In passing through them we fell in with a few natives spearing fish, and were shown a short cut which enabled us, with some difficulty, to reach the open shallow sea between the main island and the Ocean Reef some three or four miles away.

The rain now fell in torrents, and the wind came in fitful squalls sometimes so violent that we could only carry the little jib close-reefed. Beating out to the Ocean Reef, we succeeded in getting into the broad channel and, with fair wind, sped merrily along to join the *Buster* at Jamestown. We reckoned without our host. The wind increased, and often we were obliged to keep the boat away, pull down her little jib, run bare before the furious squall into the dangerous shallows, and anchor until the squall passed by. Then we rattled along once more, keeping a vigilant eye for coral patches and two or three times striking against them with very unpleasant force. The boat was in skilful hands and, thanks to Mr. Rüss, we found ourselves at a little after midnight, once more on the *Buster's* deck. Never did her little cabin look so homelike and comfortable. We found that she, too, had felt the gale, having dragged her anchors some distance towards the opposite shore.

Next day we left Jamestown for Kitè, about twenty miles to the windward, on the other side of the island. We did not anchor, but stood off and on while a boat was sent ashore to assist in bringing off what cargo might be ready. The harbour, like that of Jamestown, is very pretty, and the country quite as verdure-clad and broken. Ponapè will be a productive island some day. The soil is wonderfully fertile, but as far as I could see a great amount of terracing will be necessary. Then it will be a lovely garden, but not, I fear, till then.

The natives at the Kitè end of the island are still heathen and, like their brethren in the same stage in other islands, have no formula or settled doctrine of any kind. In superstitions, however, all the heathen of these seas abound, worshipping, or rather endeavouring to conciliate, their devils, and having a sublime faith in Booboo-men and oracles. Their kings are also priests, and have the evil eye which can bewitch or kill by lingering or sharp disease. The rite of circumcision is unknown, but they have houses of refuge for offenders and for women during the days of purification. In these and in many ways their practices curiously resemble those recorded in Bible history. In some places they preserve the skulls of their ancestors, but I am inclined to think more from affection than from any religious feeling. They believe that the son of a dead man, and he alone, can cure illness caused by the spirit of the deceased father entering the body of some one who had offended him during life. Altogether, they are a strange mixture, having much that is repellant, but with so much natural grace, good-humour, and kindliness, that the attraction is much greater, and must excite in all who have had the opportunity of seeing them, an earnest desire to further their progress toward the purer ideas and better habits for which nature has certainly fitted them.

At Kitè the heathen natives were in great tribulation. Their Christian brethren, impelled by a burning zeal in the cause of temperance, had just come in force and rooted up all their plantations of the "Piper Methisticum," from which the kava of the eastern islands (the yagona of Fiji) is made. The root requires great labour and care in cultivation, and takes long in coming to maturity. The drink made from it is refreshing. It is not intoxicating in the alcoholic sense of the term, but narcotic and only injurious when taken in great excess. Had the heathens been strong enough, they would certainly have resisted and blood feuds have followed, but their Christian fellow-countrymen were the stronger and did what they thought the work of the Lord in their own way.

To my mind, it was too much like doing evil that good might ensue, a dangerous course in civilized communities but much more dangerous and demoralizing among ignorant and uncivilized people.

At Kitè we were passed by the two whalers from Modoc Harbour to which I have before referred. Here also we were visited by two traders so opposite in character and experience, and so remarkable in their respective ways, that I beg leave to introduce them to the reader. An hour's interesting talk with these men put me up to much of the old Pacific ways in their time. The first was Mr. Begg, a quiet, reserved, and deliberate-speaking Scotchman, an engineer by trade, and an educated man. In his younger days he had lived at Mauritius and put up the first sugar-mill on that island. Thence he went to Calcutta, and took contracts for putting together the river steamers sent out in sections from the old country. Mr. Begg prospered and was on the road to fortune, when the crash of '48 came. The people who held his money failed, and he was a ruined man. Sick at heart, he realized what was left and took passage for the South Seas, finally selecting Ponapè as his future home. Gladly would he afterwards have left, but not until he had settled down to the new life did any opportunity of getting away occur.

Mr. Begg soon acquired great influence with the natives. When the American mission was established at Ponapè he rendered it great service, which the missionaries recognized by showing him kindness and attention whenever they could. He is now seventy-four years old, and a hale man still. Thirty-seven of those years have been spent at Ponapè, and "the blacksmith of Ponapè" is esteemed for his high character by all and valued for his skill in ironwork by whalers and other vessels visiting the island. Some of these facts I gleaned from himself, others from those who knew him and knew Ponapè well.

Remarking to Mr. Begg the apparent absence of good feeling between traders and missionaries, I was much struck with his reply. "Well," he said, "it is too true, and there are faults on both sides, but I hope the feeling will wear off, though I must say I don't see much sign of that at present. The old missionaries and the old traders had a strong feeling against each other, and it has come down, though less bitter now, to those who have succeeded them. In my own case I can't complain as I have not been a trader and have always been on the best terms with the missionaries. But I am afraid they won't regard me so favourably now. My teeth are gone," said the old man, with unconscious pathos, "and I can eat little but soft native food. My eldest boy is pretty good at the forge, in his way, but there is less work than in the old whaling days. My other children have also to be provided for, and so in my old age I am obliged to turn trader for their sakes. What harm," he added, "so that it be honestly done? And yet somehow I feel that the missionaries will no longer regard me with the same kindly feeling."

"Of course," he continued, "that won't affect me. I shall do the best I can for my family, but still I shall be sorry for the change." Which change of feeling, strange as it may seem, this quiet, well-informed, kindly old man looked forward to as a matter of course, and in the nature of things to be expected.

A very different man was Captain Rodd, the gentleman who came on board with Mr. Begg. A short, spare, wiry, voluble personage, over sixty years of age, full of life and action, and hard as iron. With one arm, one eye, and an ugly scar across his face, *souvenirs* of native fights in the old sandal-wood days, Captain Rodd was a character not often met with and not easily forgotten. His name figures largely in the Pacific charts as discoverer of many a reef, of several harbours, and of some small islands. An apprentice in the missionary brig *Camden*, when John Williams was killed at Erromanga, in 1839, he has a vivid recollection of the sad affair. On board were Mr. Williams, Mr. Harris an intending missionary, and a Mr. Cunningham. Williams understood natives, did not like their manner at Erromanga, and thought it would be prudent not to go ashore at once. Harris was impatient, and Williams gave way. The three passengers landed with the captain, and Harris walked in advance up a little stream. Presently he ran back, followed by a number of natives who knocked him down and clubbed him. The other two and the captain were also seen making for the boat. Cunningham and the captain got in and escaped, but Mr. Williams fell on the shingly beach and was slain. It was all over in five minutes, and a single musket-shot would have saved them. "But we had no guns in the *Camden*," said Captain Rodd, "as Mr. Williams considered it wrong for a mission ship to carry them." "Ha!" said the old man, warming up with his recollections, "Williams was a man, every inch of him. None of your d——d sanctified crawlers, like many of those who came after him. A good sailor, a good blacksmith and carpenter, a good preacher, and always ready with a kind word and helping hand for anybody, white or black. So was Bishop Patteson, whom I often had a talk with when he was left in charge at Lifu in the Loyalties. And Bishop Selwyn too. They were men. I knew them all, and have been in many a queer position, and seen many ups and downs, since that time. Sometimes making pots of money at the sandal-wood trade; sometimes at other trades. And well I know the Pacific; I should like to know who did if I don't. The sandal-wood paid best. It was a risky trade, but we were young and took our chance. We thought it would last for ever, and spent the money as fast as we made it. We had to fight sometimes. If we hadn't fought, the natives would have killed us, as they did John Williams and many another good man. Now," he asked appealingly, "I never hurt a native if I could help it, or wronged one that I know of, all my life; is that a life a man need be ashamed of? And yet no white missionary, except Mr. Logan, has ever been near me since the old days, when they used to send out real men like those I spoke about. They spurn a white man now;" and then there burst out again that shocking "d——d sanctified crawlers."

I suggested to the irascible old sailor that there was a good deal to be said on the missionary side. How, for instance, could a missionary, with perhaps a wife and family, have about him a trader not married to the native woman with whom he lived? But at this the old man fired up more fiercely than ever. "Who wants them to have our women about their families if they don't like it. As to marrying, what did the natives know about that in the old days? And, for that matter, what do they know or care now? At the same time," he added, "it was always a sore point even with Bishop Selwyn, Bishop Patteson, and men like them. But the traders had sense enough to know this; they didn't want to force themselves or their women on the missionaries. All they asked was to be treated like men when they met them." And the old man bubbled over once more with indignation at the thought. "Yes," in answer to my query, "if you write about these islands, put down by all means, what I say, if you like, and you can put my name too. Write that Edward Rodd said it—a man that never said behind another's back what he wouldn't say to his face and stand by." As we said good-bye to the two veterans and shook hands at the gangway, "I would na' back all friend Rodd's talk," said Mr. Begg; "he is a hot-tempered, peppery man, but I am bound to say there is a good deal of truth in it." I looked at the two old men as they climbed over the side and watched them to the last with great interest, for they belonged to a race becoming daily more rare. They scrambled into their boat, and we, calling out a final good-bye, braced the yards and were off for Lukunor, leaving behind us the last specimens we were likely to meet of the old trader of the Pacific, a race dying out so rapidly that the memory alone will soon remain.

Good-bye, too, to Ponapè, an island we left with great regret at not being able to give more time to the inspection of the mysterious ruins which I have, I fear, very imperfectly described. A more interesting voyage, in these hackneyed days of travel, it would be difficult to find than one to Ponapè and among the Line islands.

Only, after past experience, I should prefer to make it in a vessel supplied with auxiliary steam power. The climate, the scenery, and the novel ways of the people would render the trip, under such circumstances, one of the most enjoyable that any voyager could hit upon or undertake.

NOTE.—Since the above was written, the Spanish Governor, with a party of priests and fifty soldiers—Manilla men under Spanish officers—arrived at Jamestown Harbour and began road-making and laying out the town. This seems to have been in April, 1887, but affairs soon became so complicated that the Rev. Mr. Doane was arrested and sent by the Governor to Manilla. There the American Consul interfered. Mr. Doane was released and sent back to Ponapè with an officer, who was to supersede the Governor and act in his place. On their arrival they found that the Governor, with forty-five of the soldiers, had been killed in a quarrel with the natives. A considerable body of troops has since been sent from Manilla, but with what result I have not heard. How so disastrous a quarrel could have occurred with such a people as those of Ponapè it is difficult to understand, and the accounts that have reached us in New Zealand are too incomplete to warrant a definite opinion.

CHAPTER IX.

A CROWN COLONY OF A SEVERE TYPE.

Old Fiji—"A land of tyrants and a den of slaves"—Cakobau as a boy—His conflicts with missionaries—Commodore Wilkes at Fiji—Fijian savagery—Cakobau in 1868—The American claims—The Polynesian company—Fiji in 1869—Fijians and planters—Beginnings of government—The Fijian Crown of 1867—Government in 1869—Government finally formed (1871)—King and constitution—Meeting of Parliament (1871)—Conflict in constitution—Resignation of ministers—The Woods-Thurston Ministry—They dispense with Parliament—British subjects' Mutual Protection Society—Crown colony in 1874—Sir Arthur Gordon as governor—Degradation of the Union Jack—The blessed rule of the Colonial Office—Laying foundation for future ills—Justice to the weak.

My personal knowledge of the Fijian Islands began early in 1868, and my last visit was made in 1886, so that I am able to speak with confidence about their present condition and much of their past history. The history is fraught with interest, and not devoid of amusement.

In 1868 no government nor sign of government existed in Fiji. The population consisted of about 400 white settlers of many nationalities and 140,000 natives, of whom upwards of 100,000 were on the books of the Wesleyan Mission, and a considerable number on those of the Roman Catholic Church. A large number in the mountains were still heathen. Immigration was setting in, caused by depression in the colonies and stimulated by the high prices of cotton after the American Civil War. The paramount chief was Cakobau (Thakombau), who had subdued the coast tribes by means of his fleet of well-built war canoes, and who held an impregnable position in his little island of Bau. The heathen tribes in the mountains had only a year or two before killed the Rev. Mr. Baker, a Wesleyan missionary, who wished to cross the large island of Viti Levu. I have since heard the natives of that district declare that Mr. Baker was not eaten, and was only killed after repeated warnings. He would not return when requested or his life would have been spared, but I have already referred to this in a previous chapter.

The conversion of the natives of Fiji, and more especially of Cakobau himself, forms a curious story. Before a missionary appeared in Fiji there had arisen a party of progress, a Liberal party, if I may use the phrase. This party conceived the idea that the Fijians then living, must be more experienced and wiser therefore than their forefathers. They began to doubt their gods, and were told by white men that cannibalism was a shameful crime, that it was not practised in other countries, and that men were entitled to the possession of their own bodies with certain other natural rights of which Fijimen had not hitherto dreamed.

In the old times Fiji was literally a land of tyrants and a den of slaves. The chiefs were arrogant, treacherous, and cruel, and the lives of slaves were of no account. For example, they were killed and buried under the posts of any large building merely in honour of the chief who laid the foundation. Both men and women slaves were killed, without compunction, on the order of any chief who might wish to give a suitable feast to some distinguished visitor, or to offer human sacrifices to his gods. On a new war canoe being launched, slaves were laid across her ways and crushed to death under her keel, and on her first voyage, the crew were licensed to plunder and kill as many as they liked of other tribes, at any island at which they might touch. The manners of the Fijians were always soft and charming, but the cruelties in which they delighted in those dark times have been told in many books, and are not pleasant to write about even now.

Cakobau led the Conservative party, in the straitest sect of which he had been reared. When a child, as the Rev. Mr. Waterhouse tells us, a prisoner taken in fight was held on the ground while the boy chief beat out his brains with his own little club. Thus did the young Cakobau receive his "baptism of blood" among his savage subjects and countrymen.

The country was split into rival tribes, but Cakobau in time became paramount, and adhered rigidly to the customs of his fathers. A man of striking appearance and great natural dignity, he resisted all innovation, regarded cannibalism as a privilege of the aristocracy, objected strongly to missionaries and all innovators, and was in all things a perfect type of the Fijian noble of the olden time. The Liberals, however, gained converts, and the minds of Fijians were in ferment.

Left alone, they would probably in the course of centuries have developed a civilization of their own; but at this critical juncture the missionaries came, and after a few years of terrible anxiety, danger, and privation, made rapid progress in the islands. Many of the chiefs became converts, and with them came thousands of the common people, but Cakobau continued obdurate. Too dignified and polite to enter into a wordy conflict with the missionaries, and afraid perhaps that violence might lead to the visit of a man-of-war, he sought to wear them out. Sometimes the arms and legs of human beings, fresh from slaughter, were sent as presents with a friendly greeting from the chief. Sometimes they would find these dismal presents, without such greeting, hung over their fence on awaking in the early morning.

Through all discouragements they persevered, and at last gained a firm footing. When Cakobau's father died the heroic wives of the two missionaries (Mrs. Calvert and Mrs. Waterhouse) went to Cakobau, then called Seru, and after much trouble extorted a promise that at the funeral he would not follow the custom of his forefathers in strangling the dead chief's wives and burying them with him "as lining for the grave." Cakobau killed and buried only five. He so far gave way that while the custom of his forefathers required the sacrifice of all, he was content with only a part of the number. The customs of Fiji were terribly bloodthirsty and cruel in those days.

It is interesting to read to-day the account given by Commodore Wilkes of his visit to Fiji nearly fifty years ago. He speaks with admiration of the great canoes, some a hundred feet long, and of their magnificent appearance "with immense sails of white mats, and pennants streaming from their yards." His interviews with Cakobau's father, Tanoa, were frequent, and he tells how Tanoa came on board "almost naked, having only a small *maro* passed round his loins with long ends to it, and a large turban of white tappa, his face bedaubed with oil and ivory black, as well as his long beard and moustaches the natural hue of which was quite grey." The commodore found it necessary to warn Tanoa against further attacks on the few scattered white people in the group, and to give him good advice generally. Tanoa admitted that the advice was very good, "but he did not need it. I must give plenty to his son Seru, and talk hard to him; that he would soon be king and needed it."

When Seru came on board, it was found that he did need admonition, for although he pleased the commodore much at their first interview, "he displayed a very different bearing when he visited the ship during my absence, so much so as to require to be checked." The commodore further tells us how Seru, a short time before, had struck dead on the spot an old chief of Goro, whose only crime was not having collected the full number of cocoanuts required of him; killed the old man while he was making humble excuse and trying to give explanation. A remarkably nice young man was the Seru of those days. I must confess that I never liked him as King Cakobau, and that to my mind the child in his case proved father to the man.

The Fijians of those early times were a peculiarly savage people, cannibals of the worst description, and yet displaying the curious anomalies that strike one in these Pacific islanders. Ruthless and bloodthirsty as they were, the Fijians are among the most light-hearted, gay and pleasant of Pacific islanders. Their ruthlessness was unbounded. Few of the old stories strike one with their simple pathos more than that of the old Prussian, Martin Buschart, whose escape from a great sandal-wood fight and subsequent massacre in Fiji, led ultimately to the discovery of the fate of La Perouse. One can picture the dilapidated man " with his Fijian wife and his friend the Lascar," escaping from the slaughter to Captain Hunter's sandal-wood ship, and begging to be landed at some other island, he cared not which nor where, so long as he got away from Fiji.

There must have been some good in Buschart, or Peter Dillon, who was mate of Hunter's vessel at the time, would not have taken the trouble, when passing the island where they had landed him ten years before, to call there and see if the old man were still alive. The first to board the vessel was Buschart himself, still " with his friend, the Lascar." Through them, Dillon unexpectedly gained the clue which led to his discovery of the fate of the long-lost La Perouse, for which he was made Chevalier by Charles X., and in other ways generously rewarded.

My first acquaintance with King Cakobau was in 1868. He was then an elderly man, dignified in manner, with a drooping moustache and a slight halt from an old wound in the leg. Bau, the small island on which he lived, is only about a mile and a half round, and occupied entirely by chiefs and their slaves. He kept his great war canoes in dock at Bau, and, being within a mile of the mainland, was able at any time to attack others while his own position was impregnable. Cakobau's sway extended over nearly all the coast of Fiji, his only rival being Maafu, a Tongan chief who with some Tongan followers had settled in the Windward Islands and made himself a power there. Maafu's policy was old-fashioned and simple. Wherever two tribes fought, he sided with the weaker, helped it to put down the stronger, and then mastered both.

I first saw Cakobau in the Wesleyan church at Bau. The Rev. Mr. Tait officiated. The church was a large native building, and the people were seated on the ground, women on one side and men on the other. An old arm-chair near the pulpit was placed for Cakobau, who presently stalked in and was humbly presented by one of his attendants with a bundle tied up in a large highly-coloured cotton handkerchief. Slowly and with great dignity the king untied the parcel, took out a pair of large horn-bound spectacles, then a prayer and hymn book, and then his devotions began. Such was the man afterwards paraded by officials with much ostentation as a model of the "native gentleman," and as King of Fiji.

A few years before 1868 the Fijians had burned an American bêche-de-mer establishment. Complaint was made to the American Consul at Honolulu, and a man-of-war sent to Fiji. Cakobau went on board. The story ran that the captain asked him who was king in this country, and Cakobau proudly replied that he was. "The very man I want," was the answer. "You can tell me, then, who is to blame for this destruction of American citizens' property." Inquiry was made, and finally the King of Fiji was fined 10,000*l*., and ordered to make over several fine islands to the American Consul as security for the ultimate payment.

Years went by but no payment was made. The United States Government did not press, but the possible alienation of some of his best islands worried Cakobau greatly. Some Australian colonists stepped in. They agreed to pay this debt if Cakobau would give them 200,000 acres of land, then of no great use to him or to his people. They also asked the exclusive right to issue bank notes in Fiji and other like privileges, the meaning of which Cakobau neither knew nor cared to understand. To cement the good feeling between them he was also to be presented with a yacht and with a certain sum of money for his own immediate use. Thus was started in Melbourne the Polynesian Company, which did much to promote settlement and did good in many ways for Fiji. In 1868 the company had just been conceived, and soon afterwards the steamer *Albion* came down with the first batch of immigrants, respectable people, nearly all intending cotton planters, and with money to carry on their operations. Land was settled in every direction. Building and cultivation were actively pushed, and Fiji was started on the career which ended five years later in its becoming a British colony.

The settlers enjoyed freedom from taxes, and had many other advantages, but they pined for a regular government. They wanted a stronger sense of personal security. They wanted, above all things, negotiable titles to their land, to be able to borrow money and enlarge their operations. They desired to extend their cotton-fields while cotton was high in the market, and to establish sugar plantations as quickly as possible. At that time their only title to land was the registration of deeds at the Consulate in accordance with an engagement made by Cakobau in 1862 to recognize such registration. (See Appendix A).

Public opinion in so small and unmixed a community, consisting chiefly of planters, very effectually served the purposes of law. The settlers were chiefly half-pay officers and men of that stamp, employing Fijians, but working largely with labourers imported from other groups. These foreign labourers, as they were called, had little intercourse with Fijimen, and were relied upon by the planter to protect him and his property in case of disputes, which were always local and happily rare. One such dispute occurred at Dinka, on the Upper Rewa in 1868. Mr. Pfluger, a German, who had been long resident in New Zealand, whence he had gone to Fiji, bought a block of land from native chiefs and paid Cakobau for confirming the purchase. The natives refused to move off a portion of the land. Commodore Lambert, coming to Fiji in H.M.S. *Challenger*, was appealed to, and determined to inquire into the case. He sent a boat expedition with seventy men, but with strict orders not to land and not to fight if they could help it. Mr. Thurston, then Acting Consul and now Governor of Fiji, went with them to the disputed spot about sixty miles up the Rewa River. There the boats were suddenly and furiously fired into. They returned the fire but retreated in obedience to the orders they had received. A marine was shot through the lungs, and Mr. Kreehman, one of the Rewa settlers, of whom several accompanied the expedition unarmed, was fatally wounded. All the planters above and near Pfluger's, were obliged to retreat with the boats, and abandon their homes and the plantations they had raised with so much care and cost.

When the season came round, the natives picked the cotton from the abandoned plantations, and brought it in their canoes to sell to traders at the river mouth. They did so, at first, with tappa streaming and in open triumph. From the river banks the older planters on the lower river sometimes upbraided them as they passed, and were greeted with laughter and shouts in return. All was done with good-humour on both sides, but after a time the display of tappa and shouts of exultation were gradually dropped and the natives were content to pass down in a quieter way. In their opinion the cotton was fair booty of war, and we were not in a position to differ with them on the point.

In those earlier days quarrels were purely local. Intercourse between settlers and natives was constant, and tended to the cultivation of good feeling and to the advantage of both. Thanks to the policy pursued since Fiji became a Crown colony, the natives and Europeans now have little intercourse with each other and a dangerous gulf is widening between them. But of that more anon.

A little incident occurs to me, showing the customs of those days, and the effect of ridicule upon savages.

A number of us were one day sitting on the hotel verandah in Levuka, when there came out a native, who had just sold a wretched little chicken to the landlord. He was met by Ratu Abel, a son of Cakobau's, who swaggered up, took the sixpence from the poor wretch's trembling hand and kept it for himself. Abel was so unmercifully chaffed by the onlookers that he never tried this old Fijian custom again, at all events in presence of a European.

The gradual growth of Government in Fiji, and the abortive attempts that preceded the last successful effort, form a curious little history. The first attempt was made in 1867, but fell through. Again, in 1869, a meeting of settlers was held at Bau, to discuss the propriety of creating a Government, and formally recognizing Cakobau as king. Difficulties were in the way. Most of those present were new men, and a quaint old settler told them how they had, in 1867, drawn up a constitution and proclaimed Cakobau king, how they employed a carpenter in Levuka to make him a very handsome crown, richly jewelled with gems bought at a Levuka store, how the crown and jewels had cost four and a half dollars (eighteen shillings), and had not been paid for to that day. He warned his fellow-settlers that if they formed a Government, this was a liability they were in honour bound to take over. Undeterred by the responsibility, the meeting resolved to make Cakobau King of Fiji, and drank to his Majesty's health in a considerable quantity of the vile imitation of champagne current in the islands in those days.

His Majesty was agreeable, and a ministry was formed. I forthwith waited upon my friend and neighbour, who returned from Bau to the Rewa as Minister for Immigration, and sought his aid in getting labourers. He was obliged to confess his helplessness, as the Government had no funds, not even enough to supply him with writing paper. We had a little fun over this second attempt at forming a Government, and there the thing ended. The cause of failure was this:—The only white Layman living at Bau was one who acted as Layma's secretary there. Levuka, in the island of Ovalau, was the European centre. The Europeans had been treated kindly there by the chief, Tui Levuka, from the early days when Cakobau would have no dealings with them. To Levuka all cargo was brought, and in it a printing press and a newspaper were established. The white men had long supported Tui Levuka, and maintained him against

Cakobau, who owned only a small portion of Ovalau, and between whom and old Tui a very bitter feeling existed. Unable to raise a revenue, unable to print or circulate its laws, or to assert itself in any way at Bau, the Government again fell through, and nothing further was done except another equally abortive effort in 1870.

But the meeting of 1867, so derided in 1869, proved in the end the most important of them all. It bore unexpected fruit. The Constitution adopted at that meeting was suddenly revived in 1871, and used as authority for Cakobau's appointment of a ministry, and for calling together in his name and under more favouring circumstances a new assemblage of delegates. When originally adopted in 1867, the Constitution had been submitted to other chiefs assembled at Bau, who formally accepted Cakobau's kingship. The consenting chiefs were from Viti Levu and neighbouring islands, and were now held to the allegiance they had given. Those of the Windward group and of Vanua Levu still asserted their independence, or still looked to Maafu as their leader.

This account of Constitution-making would be incomplete without reference also to the attempt of 1870 above referred to. An abortive meeting of delegates from different parts of the group was on that occasion held in Levuka (on the 4th April, 1870) in accordance with a circular which so thoroughly explained the position that I have printed it—a rare paper now—in Appendix B. Through the rivalry between English and German settlers, this meeting ended without result. The Germans were anxious to have Maafu as king. Their business connections and influence with Tonga made them lean to him. The English and Americans preferred Cakobau whom they knew, to one whom they did not know, and they refused to recognize any one else but him.

The Government formed in 1871 proved final, and went into operation. It came about in this way. Fiji had grown, and Levuka, the metropolis and commercial centre, grew with it. Immigrants had poured in. The export of cotton in 1865 was only 9200*l*. In 1870 it was 92,700*l*. During that year the increase of white population was 1035, mostly from Australia, and therefore not so well accustomed to natives and their ways as the New Zealanders had been. The desire for legal security and negotiable land-titles was particularly strong among the new-comers. The Chamber of Commerce in Levuka, the only representative body, undertook the lighting, surveying, and improving the harbour, and similar matters. In 1870 the Chamber induced Lieut. George Austin Woods, a retired naval officer who had just resigned command of the New Zealand survey schooner, *Edith*, to come from Auckland to Fiji, and begin survey operations there. Mr. Woods completed his work, and was induced by some of the settlers to join in forming a Government. Levuka was now open to their operations, for the old Tui Levuka was dead, and his son and successor, "Sam," had an intense admiration for Cakobau. Mr. Woods was just the man they wanted, resolute, able, and genial, with a wide knowledge of the world and of colonial governments. He was sure to go thoroughly into anything to which he gave his hand, but with a strong tendency to the quarter-deck view of government and of managing mankind in general.

One morning in June, 1871, after all preliminary arrangements with influential merchants and others had been carefully made, a proclamation was issued, announcing simply

that Cakobau, Tui Viti (King of Fiji), had
been pleased, under the Constitution of 1867,
to appoint Mr. Sydney C. Burt to the Premier-
ship, and certain other gentlemen to different
ministerial offices. This was followed by the
issue of Government Gazette No. 2 (June 10th),
duly headed "Cakabau Rex," and published
"by authority." The Gazette contained an
address from the Premier to the foreign residents in Fiji, and gave a short summary of the
events that led to the formation of the Government. (See Appendix C.) A proclamation was
also issued, stating that it was desirable to
convene a meeting of delegates "from the
districts in the islands of our dominions, for
the purpose of amending the Constitution Act
assented to at Bau in the year of our Lord
1867." The proclamation further, "in pursuance of the provisions of the said Act, and by
virtue of our own authority," ordered that the
meeting should be held "at our Council Chamber, at Levuka, on the 1st day of August, 1871."
Electoral districts were created, and delegates
were returned. (See Appendix D and E.) They
met at Levuka on the day appointed, and
received a message from King Cakobau, en-
closing a Bill to amend the Constitution Act,

and another Bill for the election of representatives. These Bills were passed with various amendments, and, after being assented to by his Majesty, became law.

Fiji was now fairly afloat, with a king and a Constitution, a Ministry, a Legislative Assembly elected by the people, and a Privy Council consisting of Fijian chiefs, nominated by King Cakobau, practically a House of Lords and an integral part of the Legislature. The general election followed, and on the 2nd November, 1871, the Legislative Assembly, consisting of twenty-three members, was opened with an address from the king—of course, sent down in writing, for Cakobau was ignorant of English, except as spoken in the whale ships from which his first knowledge of its force and beauty was derived. The address must be regarded as historical, and I print it in Appendix F. The whole of these papers are valuable. They give a faithful picture of the settlers who have since been held up as only fit to be despotically governed as a Crown colony, in Lord Carnarvon's own words, "of a severe type." They show, too, how slanderous were the libels to which the settlers have since been subjected for official and selfish purposes.

The Assembly passed laws organizing various departments, and did much useful work. It sanctioned an expenditure for the ensuing year of 25,866*l*. of which sum " H.M. Privy Purse" absorbed 1500*l*., " H.M. Private Secretary," 200*l*., and " H.M. Ministers and Staff," 2500*l*. Ten native chiefs, as " Governors of Provinces," received 300*l*. each, and ten natives as " Lieut.-Governors," 50*l*. each. For the " Chief Justice and Chancellor of the Kingdom," 750*l*. was appropriated, and for a " Puisne Judge," 500*l*. A temporary loan of 5000*l*. was authorized to meet present emergencies, and the Assembly was dismissed in due form.

The Assembly had done much good and useful work, but two fatal mistakes were made. The Customs Act gave to the Government a permanent independent revenue, and another Act authorized them to raise armed forces and to discipline the same without requiring annual renewal. In effect, a Mutiny Act in perpetuity. The Constitution contained eloquent declarations about human rights, but the Assembly had deprived itself of all safeguards for their preservation.

The Constitution also contained two very faulty clauses. One prescribed that " the representation of the people shall be based on the principle of equality, and shall be regulated and apportioned from time to time by the Legislative Assembly." The other provided that "every male subject of the kingdom who shall have paid his taxes, &c., shall be entitled to vote for the representative of his district." Upon the conflict between these clauses the action of the Government was afterwards based. Of the intent there could be no doubt. The first "Assembly" had been elected exclusively by the foreign residents, and to it was given the exclusive right of regulating and apportioning the representation, leaving to Fijimen the Privy Council. But it was equally clear that the next clause gave the vote to "every male subject." Hence the conflict and the evil result which we shall presently see.

At the first Session of the Assembly several members had expressed dissatisfaction at the proposed expenditure, which they considered too large. They had no confidence also in some of the ministers, and an opposition sprung into existence. The next meeting took place in 1872, when the Assembly incorporated the town of Levuka, levied further customs duties, authorized the charter of a bank, and passed a loan bill for raising 50,000*l*., partly to pay off the previous small loan and partly for public works and general purposes. The opposition meanwhile had grown stronger. Mr. Burt resigned, and Mr. J. B. Thurston—formerly acting British Consul, but then a planter—took his place. The opposition was not satisfied, and the session ended leaving the Government weak and with many of its measures defeated, but still occupying the ministerial benches. Then the trouble began.

A rebellion had broken out among the mountaineers of the Upper Rewa, and an armed force was raised for its suppression. On the Assembly meeting in 1873, a message from King Cakobau announced that the calling together of Parliament had been deferred through ministers' attention having been engrossed with the rebellion. It also proposed, among other measures, certain amendments to the Constitution, in order to remove doubts as to the exclusive right of foreign residents to representation in the House of Assembly. An amendment to the address was carried, disapproving the policy of the Government. Then the ministers, having negotiated the loan, having an armed force, a perpetual Mutiny Act, a permanent customs revenue and revenue from other sources, dissolved the House, after tendering their resignations to his Majesty, which his Majesty of course declined accepting.

Mr. Thurston was an old resident, and spoke the language perfectly. Was it likely King Cakobau would consent to dispense with so valuable an adviser, and especially if Mr. Thurston did not wish to go? Mr. Woods too had become a "native chief," regularly *buli'd* or installed. He holds the position to this day, recognized by the natives of his district and treated by them with all the honours due to a chief whenever they meet him. Somebody outside had one day put up the Privy Council to object to the presence of "strangers" when a minister brought down a Bill from the other house for their consideration. The minister had to retire, and the channel of communication between the two Houses was thus closed. There was only one remedy, a minister must be formally made a Fijian chief and nominated to the Privy Council. Mr. Woods in due form was *buli'd* by the king and raised to the chiefdom, a rare and I think unique event in the history of this people, whose reverence for their chiefs is remarkable.

After the dissolution, ministers governed without a Parliament, holding that it would be dangerous to have new elections while Fijimen were deprived of the right to vote which the law appeared to give them, and while the white residents declared they would resist their coming to the poll if they attempted to do so. Ministers were denounced as usurpers, and people conspired and arrayed themselves against them. So, in the interests of " law and order," Ministers put two cannon in a narrow defile that separated the town from the Government buildings, and defied the opposition. As a crowning measure, they arrayed King Cakobau in a velvet knickerbocker suit and tall felt hat with moor-cock's feathers imported expressly for his Majesty from Sydney. They surrounded him with royal state and household guards, and prohibited any one approaching his Majesty except after leave duly obtained and in presence of a Minister of State.

One day, indignant at these things, the people went forth in large numbers to the "palace" at Nasova, to beg King Cakobau to dismiss his ministers or to call Parliament together immediately. They found the way barred by several hundred well-drilled native troops, officered by Europeans. The deputation moved on, and was ordered to stop, declined to do so, and was charged with fixed bayonets. Whereupon was seen the curious spectacle of a crowd of "foreign residents," English, German and American, flying pell-mell before a body of well-armed and disciplined savages. Ministers took a terrible responsibility upon themselves that day; and assuredly if Parliament had been again called together it would have been perfectly justified in impeaching and having them shot. Their clear duty in face of a defeat was to resign, and the pretext of Cakobau refusing to accept their resignation was too flimsy to conceal their own personal designs.

After this, all was turmoil, but it ended in the Secretary of State in England directing that the *de facto* Government should be recognized, and authorizing the interference of captains of men of war to prevent British subjects acting against it. Then began the organization of the settlers as "The British Subjects' Mutual Protection Society" (see Appendix G), a society which soon acquired great power, and would ultimately have ended the difficulty if English men-of-war had not interfered. As

R

leaders of this society and of the armed settlers on the Ba coast, Colonel Woollaston White and Mr. De Courcy Ireland, two Fijian planters, were deported by Captain Chapman of H.M.S. *Dido*, and carried to Sydney on the complaint and denunciation of the *de facto* Government of Fiji.

Worse than all, it was at this crisis that the *de facto* Government, in order to justify its usurpation, began to slander, and to encourage others to slander, those whose interests and whose honour should have been its first care. Ministers could only justify their action by pleading a desire to save the natives from evilly-disposed white men who wished to ill-treat and enslave them. In that character they posed. As in all conflicts of the kind, a few noisy and extreme men among their opponents rushed to the front, threatening assassination, and talking nonsense generally, but nonsense that played into their enemy's hands and was turned to account against their friends. And then, when interference by our men-of-war had come to such a pass that Germany would probably have also interfered on behalf of her ubjects resident in Fiji, the country was annexed, and on the 10th October, 1874, became a British colony. Lord Carnarvon, Secretary of State for the Colonies at the time, was pleased to say that Fiji, having been annexed, would be governed as a colony " of a severe type." For this he was loudly applauded by people who had heard the shameless slanders of Fiji and its settlers, but who knew as little about them as Lord Carnarvon did himself.

Sir Arthur Gordon, being considered, it was presumed, the right kind of man to bring to their proper bearings the evil inhabitants of the new crown colony, arrived as governor. Soon afterwards he called a general meeting at Nasova. In his opening speech he congratulated himself on finding that he had come among settlers of so high a character, and to whose welfare it would be his pride and pleasure to devote his best energies. This was said with an earnestness that filled his hearers with new hope, and made them believe that it was something more than what colonists know generally as Gubernatorial gush. But unhappily Sir Arthur had about him as chief advisers some of those who had plunged the country into difficulty, and with whose services he seems to have thought it impossible to dispense. Add to this that no governor can make himself permanently popular in a crown colony. The gulf between the governed and the governing class is too broad, and the feeling between them must grow too bitter. The rulers carry themselves as rulers. The governed resent being ruled, and the conflict is inevitable.

The people of Fiji are now struggling, as well as their weakness permits, to be emancipated from the tyranny of the Colonial Office and from the alien officials whom it sends to rule them. "Little," said an old friend whom I met in Fiji last year, as he pointed to the Union Jack flying in the governor's boat, passing us at the time, "little did I think I should ever come to regard that flag as the symbol of slavery for an Englishman. But so it is in this cursed country. We have no voice in our own affairs. The governor nominates a few men to what he calls his council. It consists of officials with a large majority, and who are always expected, when the governor tells them, to vote in a body with him. The nominated members feel themselves mere cyphers, have to come long distances at great inconvenience, get tired of attending, and at last stay away. What possible reason can there be that we should not elect at least the members who are suppo ed to be our representatives, and make them answerable to us instead of to the governor?"

What reason indeed? The same reason that kept the people of the Cape Colony in a like degrading position until Earl Grey brought their deep discontent to a head, and Englishman and Dutchman, so long at bitter feud with each other, united to obtain the self-government under which that bitterness, as if by magic, passed away. They only obtained this freedom after the grandest boycotting ever attempted—the boycotting for seven long months of a popular governor, of H.M. troops, and of the whole Government of the colony. The bitterness of those days in the Cape Colony is being repeated in Fiji. The settlers, harassed by petty and tyrannical interference, see their splendid little colony ruined by a policy which they are helpless to oppose. Hard experience forced upon old colonists in the days that are gone by the sad conviction that consideration for the poor and weak could not be expected from the Imperial Parliament. Only when strong enough to thunder over its roof and reach the ears of the people could justice be obtained. A continent lost in America, a rebellion in Canada, and very nearly another at the Cape and in Australia, were needful to shake off the government of the narrow official bureau to which Parliament consigned so many of its fellow-subjects, by whose advice alone it was guided, and whose officials scattered, and still scatter, the seeds of bitter discontent wherever they have sway.

Always too with the same excuses. In Canada the French and English, but for this beneficent bureau, would have eaten each other up. At the Cape, the Dutchman and the Englishman would have performed the same sensible operation. In New Zealand and Australia the greedy colonists would have destroyed the natives, and now in Fiji the old cry is raised once more and the old system restored.

With what result? The Fijimen, who were fast throwing off the yoke of their chiefs, are again by colonial laws brought effectively under their domination. By the same laws they are effectively prevented from working for planters, and the old kindly, growing intercourse between the white and coloured population is barred. The place of the Fijian is taken by imported Indian coolies. The planters, harassed by constant and arbitrary interference, see themselves reduced to helplessness, while the colony for which they have done so much is temporarily ruined. They see clearly the difficulty that must yet come from the introduction among the Fijian race of so many of the lowest caste of Hindoos, up to all conceivable devilry, and of whom many thousands will settle permanently in the colony. They see immigration cease and their colony avoided as though a plague were in their midst, instead of its being attractive as a very beautiful and exceptionally fertile country ought to be.

The remedy is clear and simple. Emancipate the colonists from the despotic control of an official bureau and give them an independent voice in the council of their adopted country. The tutelage in which they are kept had its origin in slander. It is an insult and an injury—a wrong that once clearly understood would be speedily redressed. The government of a Crown colony is alien to English feeling and practice, and can only be imposed on those whose weakness should be their strongest claim to consideration and their best defence against a tyranny the more galling because disguised under the forms of freedom.

CHAPTER X.

ENGLAND AND OTHER POWERS.

The "mutual" declaration—Germany's sphere—England's sphere—Unsatisfactory omissions—French missionaries—Spain as a Pacific power—French convict settlement—Origin of German claims—Johan Cæsar Godeffroi and Co—Their rise and fall—"Die Deutsche Handels- und Plantagen-Gesellschaft zum Süd-See Inseln," commonly known as the Long Handel Co.—The iron money—The "See Handels-Gesellschaft"—Prince Bismarck's guarantee—Failure to float new company—Our diplomatists—The High Commissioner—The High Court—Arbitrary powers—Judge Gorrie in evidence—Bias of the High Court—Foreign men-of-war—Cases in point—A Deputy High Commissioner—Her Majesty's ships—The Hawaiian kingdom—Tonga and her troubles—The Rev. Shirley Baker—King George of Tonga—The new National Church of Tonga—German annexation of Samoa—King Mahetou of Samoa—Braver and better counsels.

It may be presumptuous in a distant colonist to criticize the work of an eminent diplomatist like Sir Edward Baldwin Malet, her Majesty's Plenipotentiary at Berlin, but I am emboldened by the belief that I know something of the Pacific, and that Sir Edward Malet cannot, in the nature of things, know more.

When we left New Zealand (August, 1886) nothing was known of the mutual declaration signed at Berlin on the 6th April by Sir Edward Malet on behalf of England and by Count Herbert Bismarck on behalf of Germany, but I saw a copy at Jaluit, attached to the Report of the German New Guinea Company. Since my return I have also noticed a congratulatory article by Mr. C. Kinloch Cooke in the *Nineteenth Century* of November, 1886. Mr. Cooke suggests a similar mutual declaration between England and France as to their respective spheres in the rest of the Pacific. It is to be hoped that our Government will make itself acquainted with the true state of affairs before moving in that direction, or they may be led into making some serious sacrifice—surrendering, for example, Suwarrow Island, which gives us an alternative connecting link with the future canal at Panama or Nicaragua.

The declaration has secured for Germany many large tropical islands, and marked the respective limits of the German and British spheres of influence in the Western Pacific. The term Western Pacific is defined to mean that part of the ocean between 15° north and 30° south latitude and 165° west and 130° east longitude. Within this area the line of demarcation decides for each of the two powers the sphere open to its operations.

The map attached to this book will show the line, and the exact terms of the declaration will be also found in Appendix H. In addition to her portion of New Guinea, Germany acquires exclusive right to extend her protectorate or possessions over the large and fertile tropical islands of the Bismarck Archipelago, over the two most northerly of the Solomon Islands, over the Marshall Archipelago, and over several outlying islands. The inhabitants of all these islands have been annexed without their consent, and despite the certainty that their own voice would be unanimously for annexation to England or America.

Germany, in return, undertakes not to interfere with British influence on the other side of the conventional line. For this concession, if I have succeeded in making the position clear, the reader will agree with me that Britannia should bend in profoundest curtsey to the good Prince Bismarck, and thank him—for nothing.

The same declaration provides that the Navigator Islands (Samoa), the Friendly Islands (Tonga), and the Island of Niuè, shall form a neutral region. In other words, they are to continue open till the opportunity comes, and German "interests" may be used in some way to excuse the interference of the German Empire. That Germany hungers for both these groups is no secret; but I venture to think that if Germany or any other power attempts to take them, England should resist such attempt to the utmost, and at any cost. By all means let these groups maintain their independence and organize their own Governments if they can. Give them every assistance to do so. But it would indicate extreme weakness to allow any other European power to establish itself so close to Fiji, and in such commanding military positions with reference to England's great colonies.

Some few have desired to establish a Monroe doctrine and keep to ourselves what was left of the Pacific Sea, but we have already a greater extent of tropical country than we can for many years profitably occupy. It would be a poor and selfish policy to prevent others undertaking the task. Nor can the contact of great nations like France and Germany fail to bring to Australia and New Zealand much good. Their neighbourhood will tend to promote a closer union, and in that respect at all events there will be gain. The unsatisfactory part of the affair is this. If England had cause to interfere at all—if her formal recognition of Germany's acquisitions and influence were considered desirable—surely the important questions of Samoa and Tonga should have been at the same time definitely settled. Their independence at least should have been secured, and the right reserved that they might hereafter attach themselves to any nation they preferred. Instead of this, the declaration merely provides that they shall form a neutral region; in other words, be kept as they are until a pretext for hoisting the German flag can be found.

England is left at liberty to take possession of the Kingsmill and Ellice Archipelagoes, and if there be no political obstacle in other directions, it is difficult to find a reason why she should not take possession immediately. They are all atolls, and would not need a single government official, nor any expenditure beyond that incurred by the occasional visit of a man-of-war. The power to regulate the traffic in firearms would of itself be a great gain to the natives; and their unanimous consent to annexation by England could be obtained at any time without difficulty.

The fag-end of the Solomon Islands, the Santa Cruz and Banks Islands, with the New Hebrides and a few scattered islands in the Coral Seas, are all that now remain open to the extension of English influence in that part of the Western Pacific. Many of these islands are watered with the blood of English missionaries, of English sailors, and of Englishmen of all degrees who have perished in their efforts to advance the natives to a higher stage of civilization. The people are English in the fullest sense in which the term can in their case be used. French missionaries also claim their martyrs and converts in these islands, and France, with New Caledonia close at hand, may fairly consider that she has equal right with Germany to be heard in the matter.

Turning eastward, and passing by Samoa and Tonga, there is the little Tokerau (Union) group—a group of atolls already thoroughly English, and over which our flag might be raised with as little hesitation as over the Kingsmill or the Ellice Islands. There are also several scattered islands of no special value, except Suwarrow, before referred to, and all of their inhabitants are undoubtedly English in sympathy. We come then to the Cook and Austral groups. The beautiful little Cook (Hervey) group is very English, and the chiefs and people would welcome annexation at any moment. The French, from the vicinity of their own possessions as well as ours, may claim to have a voice, but surely the wishes of the natives themselves should prevail. The German Mutual Declaration has settled nothing beyond a formal recognition of the German acquisitions. Both Samoa and Tonga, the two groups with which it was most important to deal, are left in damaging doubt and uncertainty.

Spain is another European power in the Western Pacific, through possession of the great Archipelagoes of the Caroline, Ladrone, and Pellew Islands. She has held them by right of discovery for more than three centuries, and soon after their discovery several of her priests were killed in the attempt to Christianize them. Since then, Spain has attempted nothing till a year or two ago when Germany tried to snatch the Carolines from her. Shaking off her apathy, she is sending soldiers to garrison these islands, but is not likely to do anything in trade or colonization in connection with them. The Germans have a considerable trade with the Caroline Archipelago, with which Auckland and Sydney merchants have also established connection.

The French trade is confined to their own possessions, in which English and colonial traders always meet encouragement and a hearty reception. Their New Hebrides Company, for example, is a local one, formed in New Caledonia, and whose operations form the chief ground on which the French claim to the New Hebrides is based. Yet this company had for its foundation a business bought in the New Hebrides from Mr. McLeod, an island trader from New Zealand by whom that trade was established. In many respects the French are capital neighbours to a trading people like those of Australia and New Zealand; but convicts sent to their possessions are a source of bitterness which must, sooner or later, find vent. Every friendly effort is being made on the part of the colonies to end the matter. If these efforts be unsuccessful, it is more than likely that the vessels of any nation, coming from a French Pacific port, will be put into a moral quarantine, or some equally effective means, within their municipal rights, be found by the colonies to prevent the convicts gaining access to them. It is to be hoped that the great nation of France will not long allow this grievance of her colonial neighbours to impair the warm feeling of admiration and regard which the colonists have always entertained towards her.

Germany has only in recent years entered the field as a Pacific Power. An account of the origin and growth of her influence cannot fail to be interesting. For the origin we need only go back to 1857, when the well-known Hamburg merchants, Johan Cæsar Godeffroi and Company, extended their business to the South Pacific. They were an old wealthy firm, and owned many ships trading to the East Indies and China on the one hand, and to the West Coast of South America on the other. At Cochin they had a large trade in cocoanut oil, and in South America a large trade in saltpetre, cochineal, and other rich products.

At that time traders from Tahiti were in the habit of going across to Valparaiso with Tahitian produce, returning with flour and supplies for the French garrison. Mr. Anselm, the agent of Godeffroi and Company at Valparaiso, went to Tahiti in one of the vessels and, seeing the opening for business, established a branch there. Mr. Anselm was afterwards lost at sea, and Mr. Theodore Weber took his place. Under Mr. Weber's management the business was rapidly extended, and having capital at command, he soon controlled much of the Pacific island trade. In 1869 the firm advanced a sum of money to the Tongan king, securing in return nearly all the copra trade of the Tongan group. Godeffroi's head-quarters were then transferred to the more central position of Samoa. Large quantities of land were purchased, and extensive cocoanut plantations established. These plantations are now getting into full bearing, and are, I believe, among the most valuable properties possessed by the German company who took over Godeffroi's business.

At that time the islands were without sufficient coin for currency. The firm imported from South America a large quantity of Bolivian dollars, said to have been issued during one of their civil wars and afterwards called in as too debased for Bolivian use. This is the "iron money" of which one hears so much in the Pacific. It passed everywhere at four shillings to the dollar, but is not, I believe, at the present time worth more than 2s. 6d. as bullion. The missionaries strongly opposed the circulation of this currency, which the natives paid to them for the Church mission, and which they could only send at great loss to the colonies, or pay at a great discount in purchasing from casual trading-vessels. A feud sprang up between the missionaries and Godeffroi's agencies. To appease it, Herr Kegel, the general manager of the business, when making advances to the King of Tonga, agreed that not more than one half the coin circulated in Tonga should be Bolivian. No account of the currency was kept by the Tongan Government, and the concession must have been practically without effect.

Since that time new firms from Hamburg— notably the firm of Hernsheim and Co.— have entered the field. So have others from California and the colonies. They have all issued good dollars, and the circulation of the iron money is pretty well confined to a limited amount for home use in Samoa.

The advent of the wealthy and respected

firm of Godeffrois was the foundation of the German interests of which we have lately heard so much. The Godeffrois were people of large and liberal views. In buying land in Samoa their avowed intention was to found a German colony. They purposed introducing German immigrants, to whom they would sell land in moderate areas and whom they would assist at starting. It is said in the Pacific, I know not with what truth, that Johan C. Godeffroi was a schoolfellow and has always been a close friend of Prince Bismarck who showed a strong desire to help his colonizing projects. The Government of the North German Confederation gave large powers to their consul at Samoa, and the German war-steamer *Hertha*, then in China, was ordered to Samoa to aid him. The land was surveyed, arrangements were made to import mules and mule-drivers from Valparaiso and Chinese labourers from Cochin. Suddenly the Franco-Prussian war broke out and an end was put to the scheme. Curiously enough, the same war put an end to a somewhat similar, though smaller, scheme on the French side, by stopping arrangements which had been nearly concluded for the purchase by the Emperor Napoleon of the great plantations at

Tahiti, in which an Auckland firm was largely interested.

The French blockade of Hamburg and the commercial derangement of the time, involved Godeffrois in difficulty. The collapse of their Pacific trade was imminent. They obtained, it was said, from a great London financial firm an advance of 60,000*l*., on the security of their Pacific property. This enabled them to keep the numerous agencies supplied with stores and money till a new company could be formed to take up the large business they had built with so much energy and care. The company was formed, the " Deutsche Handels- und Plantagen-Gesellschaft zum Süd-See In- seln," to which I have before referred as the " Long Handle Co.," by which designation it is, in the Pacific, universally known. The business established by Godeffrois is still carried on by this company, who own the fine cocoanut plantations, and have agencies and stores everywhere.

I do not know whether this company is public or private, but in 1880 a public company under the especial care of the German Government, was originated with the view of taking over, in its turn, the business which the "Long Handle" had taken over from Godeffrois. The new company was to have the shorter title of the "Deutsche See-Handels-Gesellschaft," with a capital of 400,000*l*. The prospectus stated that the original company formed to take up Godeffrois' business (the "Long Handle") had, by letter of the 26th December, 1879, offered to hand over its enterprises to the new company, and in consideration of a guaranteed advance of 60,000*l*. from the promoters of the new company, to be repaid by the 1st October, 1880, the "Long Handle" had agreed to leave that offer open till 1st May, 1880. It further stated that the Imperial Chancellor had, by circular of 1st January, made known certain conditions (therein specified) under which he would apply to the Emperor for assistance, by a Government guarantee for twenty years of four-and-a-half per cent. on the capital subscribed.

The Imperial Chancellor, in his instructions to the Secretary of State respecting the preparation of the necessary measures (dated at Varzin, January 1st, 1880), wrote as follows: "In consequence of a well-known Hamburg firm, for reasons which did not begin with their South Sea business, having got into difficulties which threatened the South Sea trade *with the loss of what forms its centre, the factories and plantations on the Samoan Islands* [the italics are mine—F. J. M.], and in the hope that those interested would succeed with their own means in averting, in the national interest, this lamentable calamity, I believed myself in the interests of Transatlantic commerce to be justified in asking his Majesty the Emperor to grant me permission to propose to the legislature to grant the endangered interests the necessary means of existence. . . . The statute which has resulted from the various negotiations . . . offers to the smallest capitalist the possibility of participating, and by doing so of expressing the national interest in the result." The statute thus described was submitted to the German Legislature in April, 1880, and rejected. The new company fell through, and the "Long Handle" still carries on the business built up by Godeffroi and Co.

Since that time the German Government have not been inactive. The annexation of a part of Northern New Guinea (now Kaiser Wilhelm Land) was the subject of acrimonious diplomacy with our Foreign Office, diplomacy in which truth compels the admission that the German Foreign

Office had the best of it. To those behind the scenes this result could be no surprise. Prince Bismarck, it was known, had in Hamburg men on whose intimate knowledge and experience of Pacific affairs he could fully depend. It is equally well known that, with all his great responsibilities, the Prince has found time for personal interviews with men about whom our own high officials would hesitate to trouble themselves—mere skippers of trading-vessels and others of the same degree.

Our diplomatists fight, therefore, at a disadvantage. They resent, or, what is quite as bad, have the reputation of resenting as impertinence, any proffer of information from other than official sources. There is also a mischievous division of control between our Foreign and Colonial Office in these matters. It is not difficult to conceive important information sent by the governor of a Crown colony, or one of the self-governing colonies, pigeon-holed in the Colonial Office while a hot controversy may be proceeding between the Foreign Office and some other power. In fairness, it must also be remembered that Prince Bismarck has so few of these colonial eggs to hatch, whereas the nest of our Colonial Office is too full for proper care.

Kaiser Wilhelm's Land, with the large islands in its vicinity rechristened as the Bismarck Archipelago, with part of the Solomon Islands, and all the Marshall group, have been annexed during the last two years by Germany. The first-named islands are mountainous, and inhabited chiefly by savages of the Papuan race, but the Marshall Islands are all atolls, requiring no outlay for government, and entailing little responsibility. A governor for the Bismarck Archipelago has been appointed, and the New Guinea Co. administer and colonize Kaiser Wilhelm's Land with its stores of copra, caoutchouc, and valuable timber. Let us hope that Tonga and Samoa will not one day be added to the number. Most assuredly they will be if opportunity or excuse offer, unless England is prepared to make the resolute stand which their position and the universal feeling among their native people demand.

Though far from pleasant, I am bound, however, to add that there are few English colonists who would not at any time rather have to do with German or Frenchman, than

with the High Commissioners and Crown
colonial governors whom our own Imperial
Ministers have been pleased to establish as the
arbitrary rulers of their fellow-subjects who
venture to spread the commerce, and establish
the influence of England, in the lands beyond
the sea. Crown colony governors, as a rule,
are bad enough, and their existence is nothing
less than an insult to the fellow-countrymen
whom they are sent to enslave. But their
sphere is limited, while the High Commissioner
and his deputies rove at pleasure over the whole
western sea. The great abuse which the High
Commissioner was supposed to put down has
long ceased to exist. Kidnapping, which
threatened to be the curse of the Pacific, has
been long repressed by the unanimous voice of
the Australian Colonies and by the aid of five
handy little schooners of war supplied by the
Admiralty. Kidnapping has long been a thing
of the past, and needs no High Commissioner
with arbitrary powers, and no judge sitting
without a jury, for its prevention.

What other good purpose can be served by
giving to a High Commissioner and to his High
Court unchecked and arbitrary power, 'it is
impossible to say. They have no jurisdiction

over the natives, who may with impunity commit outrages on Europeans. Sir Arthur Gordon, in an official document dated March 2, 1881, makes this clear. After premising that the Western Pacific Orders in Council, and the institution of the High Commissioner's Court, have been misunderstood, Sir Arthur officially informs us that "it was not by any means to see that whites were protected from outrages by natives, and only in a secondary sense to protect natives from outrages of whites, that the Court was formed. It was principally designed to provide means for the settlement of disputes between white men themselves, and to prevent her Majesty's subjects from breaking her Majesty's laws." After so lucid an exposition, who can fail to see the great purposes the Court has to fulfil? "To prevent her Majesty's subjects from breaking her Majesty's laws," and to this end her Majesty's subjects are deprived of all Constitutional rights, treated as outlaws, placed at the mercy of despotic officials of all degrees, and deported at will to Fiji, there to be tried in a Crown colony with public opinion stifled, and with the despotic Local Government supreme. Their lives and property are further dependent on a judge sitting in his High Court alone, and without a jury. Surely comment on such a system is unnecessary.

When the Premiers of the different Australasian colonies met in Sydney at the Inter-Colonial Conference of 1881, this question of the High Commissioner and High Court was brought before them. They considered that there should be some means of appealing against the decision of a solitary judge acting without a jury, especially in cases of capital punishment. Sir John Gorrie, who presided over the High Court in Fiji at that time, attempted to refute this view in a long official reply. He admitted that it is always a great relief to a judge to know that an appeal against his decision is possible. "More especially," he adds, "must this feeling animate a judge who is obliged by the law he administers, and by the necessities of the case, to be the judge both of the facts and the law." . . . "This peculiarity of the High Commissioner's Court," continues Judge Gorrie, "would, I apprehend, be an insuperable barrier to any such appeal as proposed. . . . A trial for murder without a jury would be alien to the other colonies' system of jurisprudence, and to enable them, on appeal, to find a murderer guilty without such trial, they must have additional powers." And then, with fine humour, Judge Gorrie goes on to say that the delegates know best whether there would be any chance of passing through their respective Legislatures a Bill giving to judges such additional powers. "Moreover," adds the Judge, "unless we are to shut the door of justice on the whole native race of the Pacific as against evil-doers amongst her Majesty's subjects," ... "we must and do, under the powers of the Orders in Council, receive evidence on affirmation of those who are either not Christians or only nominally Christian, and *who do not understand the nature of an oath* in the technical sense of the English law." "This also," he considers, "would be repugnant to the proceedings of some, if not all, of the supreme courts of Australia." Well done, Judge Gorrie! Why some only? Is there one to whom it is not happily repugnant?

And how about the innocent white men butchered by the same natives, as many have been? Is there to be no thought for the widows and families of these men who are left destitute and mourning in every Australasian city, and even in your own Fiji? Has it not been laid down authoritatively that over these natives your court has no jurisdiction, and that against these natives a British subject must seek redress in vain? And, your Honour must know perfectly well that no evidence is, on the whole, so untrustworthy as the uncorroborated evidence of these natives. If you do not know this, permit me to assure you that it is a solemn fact—a fact that would be admitted by every impartial consul, naval officer, land commissioner, or missionary in Fiji and in the islands over which your Court holds despotic sway.

I have not the honour of knowing Judge Gorrie, but Fiji settlers complain very loudly that, excellent man in other respects, he has all his life been connected with Aborigines Protection Societies, and accustomed only to the peculiar ideas of governing their fellow-countrymen which are held by officials in a Crown colony. They say that on these accounts his bias is strong against them, and it must be admitted that a careful perusal of his letters on this question warrants the assertion. Still more so do his denunciations of a well-known Australian journalist, to whom he refers as being " bitter because of his failure to stir up sedition in Fiji." They leave a strong impression that in this matter of bias the Fiji people are right, and yet how tremendous is the unchecked power which the orders in council place in the hands of the judge and in the hands of a High Commissioner, who is also unfortunately human, and therefore equally prone to err.

Few of our countrymen are they who would not prefer dealing with Germans or French than with this High Court and High Commissioner. The men-of-war of both those nations are always ready to give assistance to the traders of every nationality, and this it is the simplest justice to admit. My friend Jibberik at Majuro tapu'd a trader with whom he had a quarrel, and consequently none of the natives dared to deal with that particular trader. He was an Englishman, but his complaint to the first German man-of-war obtained redress. The case was fully inquired into. Jibberik was ordered to pay 300 dollars in cocoanuts, and warned against any interference with traders in the future. He was told that if he suffered a wrong, he must take his complaint to the first man-of-war that came, just as Europeans were required themselves to do.

Majuro, in which Jibberik reigns, is German territory, but similar cases have occurred in islands unoccupied by any civilized power. On the other hand, the High Commissioner has officially stated that "the British Government disclaim all obligation to protect or interfere on behalf of persons voluntarily placing themselves in positions of danger in a savage country." The Government may interfere, but only as an act of war, for which adequate cause must be shown. Among these adequate causes a grievance such as I have referred to, however injurious and unjust, is certainly not included.

Our naval officers have happily not always accepted this *dictum*, and Majuro traders speak gratefully of the benefit they derived from good advice plainly given to King Jibberik by Captain Murray, of H.M.S. *Emerald*, and given also to other chiefs and kings. But all agree that there is an increasing hesitation, a plainly growing dislike, in our navy to incur the responsibility of interference, and to face the trouble in England which that interference has often brought upon them.

About three years ago a trader was murdered by a notorious white scoundrel at Tarawa, in the Kingsmill group. One of her Majesty's ships called soon after at Apiang, a neighbouring island, where dwelt Mr. Randolph, a friend of the murdered man, and who had formally taken his dying deposition. The murderer declared himself an American, and our captain, after mature consideration, decided that he had no right to interfere. Randolph, grievously hurt, declared that if the murderer put foot on the deck of his schooner he should certainly shoot him, but added, "I suppose, captain, you will then arrest me." "Afraid I must," was the prompt reply, "for there is no question of your being an Englishman." This story is eminently characteristic of the present position.

Some four or five years ago the *Orwell*, an Auckland vessel, was wrecked at the island of Peru, in the Kingsmills. She had a cargo valued at 3000*l*., including three tons of tobacco, five tons of rice, a great quantity of biscuit, sugar, preserved meats, and other articles. The vessel lay on the reef dry and safe when the Peru Island natives looted her, leaving literally a clean hold. Complaint was formally made to the High Commissioner, who, after considerable and damaging delay, was able to spare a deputy commissioner to look into the case. He had to proceed to Peru Island from Fiji, a couple of thousand miles away, and, after due inquiry, fined the natives thirty tons of copra (worth to them about 240*l*.), to be paid within three years from date. Natives, heathen or converted, enjoy nothing so much as a joke. They thought this a very good joke, paid the fine the first time the owners' next vessel came their way, and told the supercargo they were quite ready to get another supply at the same price.

I should weary the reader if I were to relate all the cases of which I heard on good authority, and for which redress is so hopeless that no one cares to seek it. The Germans have hitherto shown themselves as ready to protect our people as their own. Gratefully do the traders speak of this, but surely it is not a position in which Englishmen should be placed. It is weighting them too heavily in the contest —a contest growing continually more keen, and in which our countrymen will require at least as much aid from English war-ships as Germans receive from theirs. It would be a great boon if the visits of our own men-of-war were more frequent and their captains more free. Much good has resulted at various times from the rare chance visits of her Majesty's ships from the Pacific and Australian squadrons checking the aggressions to which all savages are prone. One could only wish that these visits were more regular, and that the captains were left to act more upon their own judgment after the inquiry they are able to make upon the spot.

Ruk or Hogoleu is an excellent illustration of the evil effects of vacillation in dealing with uncivilized people. The natives of this great lagoon have committed many murders with impunity. A German man-of-war called there soon after the attempted annexation of the Carolines, and the captain warned the natives against further bad conduct, saying that he would return within a year. This put them on their best behaviour for the time, but the islands reverting to Spain, the German ship did not return. Recently a Spanish war-ship arrived. She also promised to return in October last, but had not done so up to the following February, when I left Lukunor. I was assured by the Rev. Mr. Logan that this vacillation had produced a very bad effect, and a higher or better authority cannot be quoted.

England, France, Germany, and Spain are the Powers between whom the Pacific is now practically divided. Japan lately sent a warship to inquire into the murder at the Island of Lao of the crew of a Japanese trading-vessel. The Hawaiian kingdom is also in the field seeking to effect a confederation with Samoa and other of the islands. The Government of Hawaii is a Constitutional Monarchy "run" by Americans, and the country is practically American. Samoa is struggling in the agony of an effort to govern itself amid the strife caused by individual and national jealousies among the European residents. Tonga has for the present a settled Government, with King, Premier, and Parliament, which have worked till the last year or two without perceptible friction. But now Tonga is in sad trouble. A dispute on Church affairs culminated in an attempt to shoot the Premier, the Rev. Shirley Baker, as he was driving home one evening. The attempt ended sadly, for his son and daughter were with him at the time, and both were badly wounded, though Mr. Baker himself escaped. This was followed by the prompt execution, by the old King George's order, of a number of Church students alleged to have been engaged in the conspiracy, and by the banishment from Tonga of a number of other people. The Governor of Fiji, who is also High Commissioner, has gone to Tonga in H.M.S. *Diamond* with the Chief Justice of Fiji, to inquire into these troubles, or rather, I presume, into the part that may have been taken by the Rev. Mr. Baker, who comes, as an Englishman, under the Commissioner's jurisdiction. It would be improper to give an opinion while the case is *sub judice*, but a slight sketch of the position may not be uninteresting.

Mr. Baker was for many years one of the Wesleyan missionaries at Tonga but, taking part in internal politics, came into collision with the Wesleyan authorities, with whom it is a rigid rule that none of their clergy shall interfere in such matters. Mr. Baker decided to stick to politics, resigned his clerical charge, and became Premier of Tonga. The king is very old, and the premier soon acquired control of the kingdom. But great troubles are undoubtedly ahead. King George in his heathen days had many wives. As a Christian he was compelled to set all aside save one. The children of the discarded wives, though superseded, were legitimate according to native law and custom, and in native opinion the eldest has an incontestable right to succeed to the throne. Civil war is threatened, and it is notorious that the Tongans, a race of hard fighters when they fight at all—have for some time been making great preparation against King George's death.

Mr. Baker is an energetic man, as capable as most men of knowing on which side his bread is buttered and as likely as most men to endeavour to keep that side uppermost. Lately he again came into collision with the Wesleyan Church and with the French Catholic priest also. To get redress for the priests a French man-of-war was sent to Tonga. The Tongan Government wisely apologized, made the required *amende*, and so far the trouble with France ended. With the Wesleyan Church the trouble has proved more serious. The story as told to me runs thus: Mr. Baker, discovering as premier what he must have long known as a Wesleyan minister, namely, that the Wesleyan Conference in Sydney received large sums from the Tongan people, asked for an account of the expenditure. The Conference resented the demand, maintained that the Tongan Government or Premier had nothing to do with the matter, and that they were not answerable to any but the donors of the money who subscribed it of their own free will. The Conference contended, moreover, that the subscriptions were for the general service of the Mission, and not for local appropriation.

Upon this Mr. Baker—no, I should say King George—resolved to establish a Tongan Methodist Church independent of the Conference in Sydney. New churches were built, the old ones abandoned to the Conference, and the natives given to understand that it was the king's pleasure they should attend the king's new churches. Of course no penalties were inflicted nor punishment of any kind decreed, but somehow it is not found a profitable thing for a native to offend the king or go contrary to the king's pleasure in Tonga. I have heard settlers say that it is not so even in an English Crown Colony, especially with a governor who is also High Commissioner. A king must naturally be a much more formidable personage, and offending him a much more serious affair. At all events they who disregarded the king's pleasure and kept to their old churches have done very badly and come to grief in various ways. As people always will do in such cases, they have raised an "absurd" cry against a persecution which they feel keenly enough but somehow cannot legally prove. Whether the present inquiry will be more successful in eliciting the real facts than such inquiries usually are, we must patiently wait to see. Let us hope that the trouble may not end in the downfall of this promising little state and its annexation by some other power.

Let us also hope that England will forbid such annexation until at least measures have been taken to ascertain fairly and openly to what power the Tongan people desire to be annexed. They are perhaps the finest race in the Pacific, and with ordinary fair play are sure to improve rapidly. Their time of trouble is at hand, for the old king is nearly imbecile, and cannot last much longer. Their friends must hope that they will surmount that trouble and retain their independence. Failing this, they will look to England, and the Tongans will themselves look to England as their oldest, most natural, and most trusted friend. They will trust her to see that they have at least a free voice in deciding to what civilized power they shall be attached.

As with the Tongans, so with all the native races in the Pacific. Conscious of their own weakness, they look to England, and place their trust in her support. They know that, despite many blunders and occasional individual wrong, her aims are high and her people mean to be considerate and just. It is a noble position and one of which a great country may well be proud. Every true Englishman, home-bred or colonial, will pray that this proud position England may ever merit and maintain.

Here I had ended my sketch of the Old Pacific and the New. Since it was written events have happened in Samoa which can only be referred to with pain and deep regret. Picking a quarrel on the most frivolous pretexts, the German squadron rendezvoused at Samoa. A large armed force was landed, and the King (Malietoa), a staunch upholder of English influence, and openly supported by the High Commissioner and British Consul, was dethroned and deported to the German possessions in Eastern Africa. Another chief (Tamasese), a mere tool of the German residents, was installed, and is now maintained by

an armed German force in Malietoa's place.
Our Government has remained quiescent
throughout these strange events, and according
to appearances the German Government
must have acted on another "mutual" understanding.
If so, a grave error has been committed,
a grave blow struck at our influence
with the natives, and the seed of much future
trouble sown. The Government of the United
States has been equally quiescent, but they
have for some years held a lease from the
native king, for a valuable coaling-station in
Samoa, which no doubt they will continue to
hold whatever form the government of the
country may take. Colonists, still sore from
the official blundering which gave the North
of New Guinea so carelessly to Germany,
regard the proceedings in Samoa with angry
surprise and with a pain which only they who
know their pride in the country of their fathers
can understand. Willingly and gladly would
they have perilled all they possess to aid
England in maintaining for herself and for
them the position she has so well earned and
has so good a right to claim. Let us hope
that braver and better counsels will yet prevail;
this timid and dangerous policy be dis-

carded. Let Germany be plainly told that if it is worth her while to fight for Samoa it is worth ours to resist her, and that, if the Natives find it impracticable to govern themselves, we intend to secure for them a free and full voice in deciding upon the nation to which they shall belong.

APPENDIX A.

SHOWING HOW LAND TITLES WERE REGISTERED IN FIJI IN 1862.

THE following documents show the mode in which titles to land were originally acquired and registered in Fiji:—

Ko i au na Vuni Valus, au sa vakadonuia na vanua ni Kai Papalagi i Viti na Vanua sa vakadonuia i na vale ni Konisela Peretania. Au sa vola oqo e Levuka, Ovalau.

2 *Apirila*, 1862.

E. CAKOBAU,
X
VUNI VALU.

VAKADINADINA,
    WILL. T. PRITCHARD, *H.B.M. Consul.*
    CHAS. WISE, *Consular Interpreter.*
Witnesses to mark of Cakobau,
    JAMES CALVERT,
    J. M. BROWER, *U.S. Consul.*

[*Translation.*]

I, the Vuni Valu, do confirm the lands of the foreigners in Fiji—the lands that are confirmed in the office of the British Consul.

    LEVUKA OVALAU,
2 *April.* 1862.

come to the English markets, if such markets will pay best to the importers of produce.

It does not consider that any advantage is to be derived from interfering in colonial politics.

Such being the case, it is very unlikely that it will spend British money upon any new dependency, such as this would be.

The American Government holds views very similar to the British Government, and though anxious to protect trade and enterprise of every legitimate kind, is unwilling to weaken itself by having to protect positions so far removed from the centre of its Government.

The French have obtained possession of some of the most fertile islands in the South Seas whose commercial and military positions are unrivalled, whose harbours cannot be surpassed for the use of warlike fleets or ports for merchant shipping. Thus, it is not likely that their Government will incur further expense by taking possession of these islands; nor do we consider that it would be desirable that the strong, and perhaps arbitrary measures adopted towards the natives and original holders of the soil in New Caledonia, should be adopted or would be most beneficial to a white population settling in Fiji.

The other continental governments, we know, have their hands full, and are not likely to be able to lend us any extraordinary assistance towards securing our properties in the group.

It must thus appear that we are in an excessively unprotected state, far from our native homes, having brought with us our families and fortunes; and although we have made more room for those we have left behind, we not only receive no thanks, but we also receive no assistance in the somewhat perilous career which most of us have undertaken.

The consuls have their hands tied by their governments, and are thus unable to afford us any practical protection, the promise that they will see into any affair which may arise between ill-disposed savages and ourselves when a man-of-war arrives, is but poor consolation to the man whose wife has been assaulted, whose children have been injured, whose property has been destroyed, and who, after several years of labour in a tropical climate for the good, not only of himself and family, but of Europeans in general, finds himself injured, wounded, and penniless, and, to add to the sum of his evils, slighted by his consul and offered a passage home as a destitute subject.

On this head it is only necessary to add that the respect hitherto partially shown by natives towards white men is daily decreasing. The time has come when it behoves all of us to consider well our precarious position, and to take such steps as will enable us to offer a better security to all commercial people in the colonies, and to secure for ourselves permanently the advantages and profits which must accrue from cultivating under proper auspices those lands which we have rightfully acquired.

(2.) We can soon expect answers to the numerous petitions that have been sent to different governments; and, considering their answers, find out whether we may not decline, with thanks, receiving any more of their insignificant protection; and it will be well to ascertain whether foreign powers will not show more respect to us as an independent community, well regulated in its internal government, and observing justice to all, natives and outsiders, and strictly looking into the commercial integrity of those trading in this group.

The public are informed, on fair authority, that the commanders of American war-vessels would recognize and respect any self-governed community, professing the same principles of liberty and justice which are now respected in the United States, and we have no doubt that though the community proposed to be constituted will consist of the sons of many nations, the American Eagle will spread its protecting wings over a body of honest, resolute, and enterprising men.

(3.) Under the third head we announce the most important part of the proposed plan, and begin by stating the probable result of advanced steps being taken by the community. We have been led to believe, and we hope rightly, that there are some 2300 white inhabitants of this group. We are sure that from this number 1000 can be found worthy of the name of men in the highest acceptation of the word. Men who have come here bent upon making a pleasant but honest livelihood, and acquiring properties which they will be able to leave in a flourishing condition to their successors, and which they may feel sure shall be secured to them by their present toil and energies. Amongst this 1000 men we may hope to find persons suitable, and commanding zeal enough to be chosen to form a governing committee uninfluenced by pecuniary motives; and to whom, having been duly elected, the community will show all allegiance and all proper obedience, without allowing private affairs or personal jealousy to interfere.

If such a committee—with an universally balloted-for president—were elected, should a wrong or an outrage then be committed upon any one, who, relying upon the integrity of the community, has signed allegiance to its governing power, let him then appeal for protection and redress to that governing power; and it will, having satisfied itself of the facts of the case, call together a sufficient number of the community, bounden to obey its orders, and proceed at once, at public expense, to redress the wrongs of the applicants.

The president, with the approval of the committee, will appoint a suitable person to take command of such an expedition, whose duty it will be to control those under his orders, at his own responsibility, and to inflict such punishment as he may deem fitting, after reviewing the nature of the offence on the ground where the outrage has been committed.

Having so far, in this preliminary appeal to your assistance, stated the self-protectory object we have in view, we may give you our ideas of the capability of fifty or 100 men to punish any aggressor, be he a powerful or a petty chief in Fiji. In all cases a large preponderance of natives will always be on our side, and it is not to be doubted, that though a failure attended the principal attempt on the part of a small British force to avenge injuries sustained by their fellow-countrymen, fifty gentlemen conversant with the habits of Fijians, and acquainted with the manner of their tracks and fortifications, would have no difficulty in expelling them from their most secure strongholds.

Much also might be effected without violence, by the mere presence of determined and well-armed white men. There can be no doubt, also, that less bloodshed would ensue by a strong, though inoffensive militia being always ready and at hand to support their own just rights, as well as those of the persons who will join with them in the cost and risk of self-protection.

(4.) It will be proposed to you at the general meeting that a capitation tax of 2*l*. per annum be levied by this community to defray expenses. We believe that, taking into consideration the number of white residents, this subscription will be found amply sufficient to cover the cost of boats, munitions of war, stores, &c., necessary for use in order to quell any disturbance which might arise, and to defray the expenses of calling and mustering the force required. It will also be understood that every person seeking the protection of this community will be bound to supply any boats or other articles wanted by the committee for an expedition of the sort alluded to above, the committee compensating the owner of such property at the current rate.

(5.) Lastly, we propose that—

Thursday, the 14th of April, 1870,

be appointed the day for the general meeting to be held at Levuka, to which all people, whether desirous of furthering these views or not, are requested to attend; that men in different parts of the group, who by peculiar and extraordinary circumstances may be unable to be present, will authorize such of their friends (as they may think fit, and who are coming), by written and attested authority to sign for them any document agreed to by the majority. As such a large gathering of white men might alarm the natives who would not

Appendix. 293

understand its object, we think it advisable that you bring with you your personal arms in as unostentatious manner as possible.

    Archibald W. Hamilton, Taviuni.
    J. Cobban Smith, Levuka.
    Alexr. Barrack, Savu Savu Bay.
    Otty Cudlip, Levuka.
    Rupert Ryder, Mango.
    George Rodney Burt, Kandavu.
    Beamish Fitzgibbon, Suva.
    R. M. Wilson, Wainunu:
    J. Newmarch, Rewa.
    Theodore Yates, Rewa.
    Thomas Grover, Levuka.
    M. F. Ignacio Lardelli, Levuka.
    F. Hennings, Levuka.
    G. Hennings, Rewa.
    W. Hennings, Lomo Lomo.
    J. F. Wilson, Taviuni.
    Wm. Reece, Levuka.
    Joseph Glenny, Levuka.
    Geo. H. W. Markham, Nadi.
    Henry Tucker, Nadi.
    Geo. A. Carstairs, Taviuni.
    W. M. Kinross, Tai Levu.
    James Perkins, Levuka.
    Geo. Derby, Ta na Vusa.
    Thos. King, Nadroga.
    Richard D. Bentley, Rewa.
    Wm. Robertson, M.D., Levuka.
    Alex. H. Woodside, Rewa.
    Robert Spowart, Levuka.

Alfred J. Cripps, Raki Raki.
Wm. Stoneham Morgan, Levuka.
Wm. Chapman, Levuka.
P. Thagaard, Kaimba.
J. Muller, Kaimba.
Robert Morgan, Levuka.
Nathaniel Chalmers, Rewa.
J. Spiers, Rewa.

APPENDIX C.

GOVERNMENT GAZETTE OF JUNE 10, 1871, CONTAINING OFFICIAL NOTIFICATION OF THE CONSTITUTION OF A GOVERNMENT UNDER KING CAKOBAU.

EXTRACTED from the second Gazette issued by Cakobau's government, and explaining the mode in which the Government had been formed:—

TO THE FOREIGN RESIDENTS IN FIJI.

Ministers think it advisable that they should now offer some explanation of the causes that led to the appointment of the executive by the king.

First.—The largely increasing European population.

Second.—The growing want of confidence in commercial matters.

Third.—The loudly expressed hesitation of merchants and capitalists in the colonies to deal with investments in Fiji until a form of Government had been adopted, together with the advent of a mail postal service from the Australian colonies to America, making Levuka a port of call, necessitating public works of some magnitude, to ensure the safe and perfect navigation of these waters, and the fact that 300*l.*, the cost of the preliminary works lately undertaken, was subscribed by five individuals in Levuka, led to a consultation with Cakobau for the purpose of inducing him to place aside funds or securities to carry out the object sought.

Cakobau, after much thought, saw no way out of the difficulty, except by the formation of a Government in conformity with the Bau Constitution of 1867.

A member of the present executive, after much persuasion, undertook the responsibility, upon the *express understanding* that no public meeting was to be called. Cakobau's experience of such meetings only leading him to believe in repeated failures, and entire want of co-operation amongst the white residents.

With much reluctance the gentlemen named in the king's proclamation of the 5th inst., accepted office, upon the condition that they were to be at liberty to amend the Constitution in such a way as to render it acceptable, and adapted to the altered circumstances and requirements of the islands. In furtherance of which you will by reference to the *Government Gazette* of this date, notice that delegates have been summoned to meet at Levuka on the 1st of August, the earliest date possible consistent with the widely scattered districts, the present uncertain communication, and the time necessary to make the elections.

Thoughtful men must admit the necessity of a system of responsible Government, the want of a revenue for public benefit, the adjustment of titles to land, and the other important matters referred to in the king's address.

Taking then all these matters into consideration, the daily reproach of the colonial newspapers upon our supposed lawless state, the refusal of Great Britain and the

United States to accept a cession of the islands, the want of unanimity amongst the foreign residents, left no course open but the one adopted.

Ministers have accepted office with a full knowledge of the deep responsibilities they incur, and that in the exercise of their functions they consider themselves as much your representatives as the king's advisers.

They ask, therefore, your consideration; promising that, until a House of Representatives be assembled, no matters, except of urgent public necessity, will be initiated.

Ministers are fully aware of the erroneous impression existing in the minds of many European residents respecting the right of the Vuni Valu to assume the title of King of Fiji, and for general information publish in the *Government Gazette* a document, from which it will be seen that every ruling chief in these islands has acknowledged Cakobau to be their sovereign ruler, and has sworn allegiance to him in the most solemn manner.

SYDNEY CHARLES BURT, *Premier*.

Government Offices, Levuka,
    June 9th, 1871.

APPENDIX D.

PROCLAMATION OF JUNE 9, 1871, REVIVING THE LAPSED CONSTITUTION OF 1867, AND CONVENING A MEETING OF DELEGATES FOR AUGUST 1, 1871.

CAKOBAU TUI VITI.

WHEREAS it is desirable that a meeting of delegates from the districts in the islands of our dominions should assemble at our town of Levuka, in the island of Ovalau, for the purpose of amending the Constitution, Act, assented to at Bau, in the year of our Lord, 1867.

In pursuance of the provisions of this Act, and by virtue of our own authority, we do, by these presents, convene a meeting of delegates from the districts in the schedule hereunto annexed, requesting foreign residents to return delegates in accordance with such schedule, to meet at our Council Chamber, at Levuka, on the 1st day of August, one thousand eight hundred and seventy-one.

Issued and passed at our Council Chamber, at Levuka, this 9th day of June, 1871.

CAKOBAU.
SYDNEY CHARLES BURT, *Premier.*

Districts for the Return of Delegates.

Ba.—Two members.

Comprising the coast line of Viti Levu and islands adjacent between Ba Passage Point, in long. 177° 22′ E., and the Island of Rakiraki in long. 178° E.

And so on for ten other districts, defined in the schedule, each sending one member.

Ovalau four members, and two other districts two members each—in all fourteen districts and twen'y delegates.

APPENDIX E.

OATH OF ALLEGIANCE TO CAKOBAU BY 297 CHIEFS IN 1867.

EXTRACT from same Fijian Government Gazette, showing position asserted by Cakobau with reference to a large number of the other chiefs of Fiji, at that time, under the Constitution of 1867:—

Bau, May 27th, 28th, 30th, 1867.

We, chiefs of the Kingdom of Bau, do make oath as follows:—.

I swear before God that I will uphold and support the authority of the King, the Constitution, and the laws of Bau.

> Ko Mai, Na Ua, Mai Koro, Ko Mai, Bau Bau, Mai Bau, Ratu Savenaca Mai Bau, and 294 other chiefs and subordinate chiefs of various tribes in Fiji.

I, Samuel A. St. John, solemnly and sincerely declare that on the 27th, 28th, and 30th days of May, in the year 1867, while acting as Secretary of State Commissioner, Cakobau, King of the Bau Dominions, did, on the above date, administer the oath of allegiance to the chiefs each and separately, whose names and marks are foregoing, being assisted therein by Mr. W. H. Drew, their obligation, and the consequences of breaking same being fully explained to them before signing.

(Signed)   S. A. St. John.

I, William Hoskins Drew, hereby solemnly and sincerely declare that I assisted Mr. S. A. St. John, in administering the oath of allegiance to the chiefs, whose names and marks are foregoing, that their marks were made willingly, publicly, and without coercion, and that the constitution and laws of the Bau kingdom were read to them in the native language before signing.

(Signed)   W. H. Drew.

APPENDIX F.

KING CAKOBAU'S ADDRESS AT THE OPENING OF THE FIRST PARLIAMENT, Nov. 3, 1871.

To the members of the Legislative Assembly, Gentlemen,—It is to me a matter of no ordinary gratification to welcome here to-day my first Parliament, and I am pleased to remark the presence of many gentlemen who responded to my invitation to establish the constitution, which is now happily the law of the land.

Upon you, gentlemen, rests the responsibility of framing under that constitution such judicious laws and regulations as will ensure harmony between native and foreign residents, foster commercial enterprise, develop the resources of the islands, and attract to our shores energy, skill, and capital from other countries.

My advisers will lay before you a carefully compiled code of laws for the administration of justice in a simple form; and the establishment of a supreme court and provincial courts.

A first necessity will be the appointment of a municipal commission for the town of Levuka, to improve the sanitary condition, provide water supply, proper roads, and convenience for traffic, the want of which is much felt, and rendered imperative by the daily increasing population.

The labour question has had my serious consideration, the report of a commission appointed to take evidence and inquire generally into the subject will be laid before you.

My efforts have been directed to supply planters with Fijian labour upon terms beneficial equally to planter as well as labourer, the regulations for which I leave to your careful consideration.

By this measure the country will be relieved from the drain upon its resources, inseparable from the cost involved in the introduction of foreign labour.

The many difficulties attendant upon the adjustment of titles and claims to land will, I trust, be solved by the measures submitted for your approval. Your attention will also be directed to an act for the better regulation of sales, and the management of native and waste lands.

With regard to the appointment of magistrates my executive advise that the issue of a commission of the peace be deferred until the conclusion of your deliberations.

There will be laid before you details for a postal department, and the establishment of a mail service throughout the group.

It has also been considered advisable to place a sum on the estimates as a subsidy towards an ocean mail service between the Australias and the Continent of America, calling at Levuka.

The large sum withdrawn from circulation by the native community, who are reserving it for payment of taxes, coupled with the want of banking accommodation and a proper circulating medium, has been much felt. Temporary and safe measures to relieve the immediate pressure have, however, been taken by my government.

The state of matters on the Ba coast has given me much anxiety. One of my advisers, in company with the governor of the province, has visited the district, and made himself personally acquainted with the position of affairs. For the immediate protection of white settlers, a force of paid native police has been stationed at the most assailable and insecure points.

You will be asked to vote a sum sufficient to organize and equip a force equal to the protection of the white residents, although I fear that in the interim the expedition to the mountains,[1] undertaken against my advice, will provoke the mountaineers to prepare for war and cause the white settlers to be continually on the defensive.

You will notice that I have considered it necessary to prohibit the landing of arms or ammunition on any part of Viti Levu.

With a single exception the ruling chiefs of the group have tendered me their allegiance, and are now members of my Privy Council; but the assurances I have received from the chief in question, leads me to infer that personally he desires to, and shortly will assume his rightful position in my kingdom.

Large claims having been made on my Government by the United States Consul on behalf of American

[1] This must have referred to the expedition sent by Commodore Lambert per H.M.S. *Challenger*.

citizens resident at Cakadrovi, rendered it necessary that two members of my executive, in conjunction with the Consul and the Commander of the United States' corvette *St. Mary's,* should proceed to Wairiki, and seek an interview with the chief of Cakadrovi; the result of that interview I feel confident will tend to diminish native interference with white residents. I regret that the importance of this matter necessitated a short delay in calling you together.

The public recognition of my position by the naval representatives of foreign powers recently in these waters, must be not only gratifying to those who have the interests of the kingdom at heart, but affords assurance that the Treaties submitted for the consideration of foreign powers will be assented to.

The action taken by the majority of foreign residents in support of my Government evinces a desire for law and order highly commendable.

There will be submitted to you measures for raising the revenue necessary for the government of the kingdom, and you will be asked to vote supplies for the nine months ending on the 1st day of July, 1872.

Under Divine Providence I now entrust to the wisdom of your councils the affairs of my kingdom, feeling assured that there will be given to each measure the thought and consideration required to establish my Government on such a sound basis as will not only prove beneficial to the interests of my subjects, but secure the respect and approval of the civilized world.

CAKOBAU, R.

APPENDIX G.

SECRET CIRCULAR INVITING TO THE FORMATION OF A BRITISH SUBJECTS' MUTUAL PROTECTION SOCIETY TO OVERTURN A USURPING MINISTRY BY ARMED FORCE, IF NECESSARY (Jan. 20, 1873.)

(Copy of the document secretly circulated, to form an association for the deposition of Cakobau's Ministers, and which constituted the chief ground for the deportation to Sydney of Colonel Woollaston White):—

Memoranda for the information of the Settlers on the Rewa.

Mem. 1.—At a meeting held at Keyse's Hotel, on the 18th day of December, 1872, it was resolved "That a Society be formed, with a view of deposing the present Government."

Note 1.—This meeting was called because some of us saw plainly, from the Acts of the Government, that the country would be so deeply plunged into debt as to prevent our being annexed. The Home Government would not take up a debt of an unreasonable amount, and we should be unable to pay any very large amount ourselves.

Note 2.—The Government have broken the Constitution Act whenever it suited their purpose.

(See Clauses 46 and 61.)

Mem. 2.—At the same meeting it was decided, after a long discussion, that the Society be called "The British Subjects' Mutual Protection Society."

Mem. 3.—On the next day those present at the meeting (fourteen) signed this pledge: "We, the undersigned settlers in Fiji, hereby pledge ourselves to mutual assistance, in our determination to depose the present Government with a view to the future annexation of Fiji to Great Britain, and the immediate reduction of the unreasonable expenses of the present administration."

Here follow the signatures, now increased from fourteen to forty-six, not including Ba, Nadi, and Nadroga.

Mem. 4.—A Committee was appointed to canvass in Levuka for persons willing to subscribe the above pledge. The committee, consisting of White, Keyse, Beatson, Weeker, Townsend, Baily, E. S. Smith, and Fullerton.

Note.—It is now so evident, in spite of the opinion of Mr Thurston, that the country, almost to a man, is desirous of annexation and retrenchment, that we hope local Committees will be formed, who will work heart and hand with the Society at its headquarters.

Mem. 5.—T. W. White was appointed President, H. J. Beatson, Vice-President, and James Fullerton, Secretary of the Society.

Mem. 6.—It was resolved that at the meetings of the Society members only be admitted, and, to secure that what may pass at those meetings shall not be divulged, an oath of secrecy shall be taken, and a sign and password used.

Note.—Since this resolution those members who have been able to attend meetings have taken the oath of secrecy—they number 37 out of 46.

Mem. 7.—The President is authorized to charter the steamer, *Pride of Fiji*, when he considers it necessary for the good of the Society.

Note.—For this purpose £50 is collected, and subscriptions are solicited.

Mem. 8.—The Central Committee are also authorized to charter two vessels, one to go to Taviuni, and the other to Vanua Levu. Each vessel to be in charge of two members of the Society. This is for the purpose of explaining more fully to outlying settlers the object of the B.S.M.P. Society.

Mem. 9.—On January 6th, 1873, it was resolved "that the President of the Society invite a deputation from every district in Fiji to meet in Levuka on the 10th day of February, to consider the present state of political affairs in Fiji." This invitation, it is hoped, will be responded to. I trust that these notes will show pretty clearly the intentions of the Society. I also trust that the settlers of the Rewa district will become members of the Society, and will, in conjunction with others, show that they will not be imposed upon by a few men who habitually break their promises to their constituents and the public generally, and who further show by their actions that they are only influenced by motives of self-interest, and to attain their ends will use any means in their power, no matter how despotic, cruel, or unjust.

(Signed) THOMAS WOOLLASTON WHITE,
President B.S.M.P. Society.

Levuka, 20th January, 1873.

APPENDIX II.

CONVENTION BETWEEN GREAT BRITAIN AND GERMANY AS TO SPHERES OF RESPECTIVE INFLUENCE IN THE WESTERN PACIFIC (April 6, 1886).

DECLARATION between the Governments of Great Britain and the German Empire relating to the demarcation of the British and German spheres of influence in the Western Pacific. (Signed at Berlin, 6th April, 1886.)

The Government of her Majesty the Queen of the United Kingdom of Great Britain and Ireland, and the Government of his Majesty the German Emperor, having resolved to define the limits of the British and German spheres of influence in the Western Pacific.

The undersigned, duly empowered for that purpose, viz. (1) Sir Edward Baldwin Malet, her Britannic Majesty's Ambassador Extraordinary and Plenipotentiary; (2) Count Herbert Bismarck, his Imperial Majesty's Under Secretary of State for Foreign Affairs, have agreed, on behalf of their respective Governments, to make the following declaration:—

1. For the purpose of this declaration the expression, "Western Pacific" means that part of the Pacific Ocean lying between the 15th parallel of north latitude and the 30th parallel of south latitude, and between the

Appendix. 311

165th meridian of longitude west, and the 130th meridian of longitude east of Greenwich.

2. A conventional line of demarcation in the Western Pacific is agreed to, starting from the north-east coast of New Guinea, at a point near Mitre Rock, on the 8th parallel of south latitude, being the boundary between the British and German possessions on that coast, and following that parallel to point A, and thence continuing to points B, C, D, E, F, G, as indicated in the accompanying charts, which points are situated as follows:—(A.) 8° south latitude 154° longitude east of Greenwich. (B.) 7° 15' south latitude, 155° 25' east longitude. (C.) 7° 15' south latitude, 155° 35' east longitude. (D.) 7° 25' south latitude, 156° 40' east longitude. (E.) 8° 50' south latitude, 159° 50' east longitude. (F.) 6° north latitude, 173° 30' east longitude. (G.) 15° north latitude, 173° 30' east longitude. The point A is indicated on the British Admiralty Chart 780 Pacific Ocean (south-west sheet); the points B, C, D, and E are indicated on the British Admiralty Chart 214 (South Pacific Solomon Islands); and the points F and G on the British Admiralty Chart 781, Pacific Ocean (north-west sheet).

3. Germany engages not to make acquisitions of territory, except protectorates, or interfere with the extension of British influence, and to give up any acquisitions of territory or protectorates already established in that part of the Western Pacific lying to the east, south-east, or south of the said conventional line.

4. Great Britain engages not to make acquisitions of territory, except protectorates, or interfere with the

extension of German influence, and to give up any acquisitions of territory or protectorates already established in that part of the Western Pacific lying to the west, north-west, or north of the said conventional line.

5. Should further surveys show that any islands now indicated on the said charts as lying on one side of the said conventional line are, in reality, on the other side, the said line shall be modified so that such islands shall appear on the same side of the line as at present shown on the said charts.

6. This declaration does not apply to the Navigator Islands (Samoa), which are affected by treaties with Great Britain, Germany, and the United States; nor to the Friendly Islands (Tonga), which are affected by treaties with Great Britain and Germany; nor to the Island of Niué (Savage Island), which groups of islands shall continue to form a neutral region; nor to any islands or places in the Western Pacific which are now under the sovereignty or protection of any other civilized power than Great Britain or Germany.

Declared and signed in duplicate at Berlin, this sixth day of April, 1886.

(L.S.) EDWARD B. MALET.
(L.S.) Graf. BISMARCK.

Declaration between the Governments of Great Britain and the German Empire relating to the Reciprocal Freedom of Trade and Commerce in the British and German possessions and protectorates in the Western Pacific. (Signed at Berlin, 10th April, 1886.)

The Government of her Majesty the Queen of the

United Kingdom of Great Britain and Ireland, and the Government of his Majesty the German Emperor, having resolved to guarantee to each other, so soon as the British and German spheres of influence in the Western Pacific have been demarcated, reciprocal freedom of trade and commerce in their possessions and protectorates within the limits specified in the present declaration, the undersigned, Sir Edward Baldwin Malet, her Britannic Majesty's Ambassador Extraordinary and Plenipotentiary; and Count Herbert Bismarck, his Imperial Majesty's Under Secretary of State for Foreign Affairs, having been duly empowered to that effect, have agreed, on behalf of their respective Governments, to make the following declaration:—

1. For the purpose of this declaration the expression "Western Pacific" means that part of the Pacific Ocean lying between the 15th parallel of north latitude and the 30th parallel of south latitude, and between the 165th meridian of longitude west, and the 130th meridian of longitude east of Greenwich.

2. The Government of her Britannic Majesty and the Government of his Majesty the Emperor agree that the subjects of either State shall be free to resort to all the possessions or protectorates of the other State in the Western Pacific, and to settle there, and to acquire and to hold all kinds of property, and to engage in all descriptions of trade and professions, and agricultural and industrial undertakings, subject to the same conditions and laws, and enjoying the same religious freedom, and the same protection and privileges, as the subjects of the Sovereign or protecting State.

3. In all the British and German possessions and

protectorates in the Western Pacific the ships of both States shall, in all respects, reciprocally enjoy equal treatment, as well as most-favoured-nation treatment, and merchandise of whatever origin imported by the subjects of either State, under whatever flag, shall not be liable to any other or higher duties than that imported by the subjects of the other State, or of any third power.

4. All disputed claims to land alleged to have been acquired by a British subject in a German posssession or protectorate, or by a German subject in a British possession or protectorate, prior to the proclamation of sovereignty, or of protectorate by either of the two Governments, shall be examined and decided by a mixed Commission, to be nominated for that purpose by the two Governments. The claim may, however, be settled by the local authority alone, if the claimant to the land makes formal application to that effect.

5. Both Governments engage not to establish any penal settlements in, or to transport convicts to the Western Pacific.

6. In this declaration the words "possessions and protectorates in the Western Pacific" shall not include the colonies which now have fully-constituted Governments and Legislatures. The present declaration shall take effect from the date of its signature.

Declared and signed, in duplicate, at Berlin, this tenth day of April, 1886.

(L.S.) EDWARD B. MALET.
(L.S.) Graf. BISMARCK.

APPENDIX I.

STEAM LINES NOW AT WORK BETWEEN EUROPE AND THE VARIOUS COLONIES AND SETTLEMENTS IN THE PACIFIC.

THE following list of steam companies, culled from the advertisements in various Australian and New Zealand newspapers, will give an idea of the life now animating the larger Pacific centres, and extending rapidly to all parts of the Ocean. The French Company (Messageries Maritimes), and the German Company (Nord Deutscher Lloyd's), have only recently extended their operations to the Pacific. Their steamers, and those of many of the other companies mentioned have a European celebrity. The Union Steam Shipping Company's splendid line from Francisco is also well known, and the steamers of the direct lines to New Zealand range from 3500 to 5000 tons:—

LONDON TO AUCKLAND AND OTHER PORTS OF NEW ZEALAND.

Union Steam Shipping Company, *viâ* San Francisco, calling at Honolulu (Hawaii) and Samoa.

New Zealand Shipping Company, monthly steamer,

viâ Cape of Good Hope, calling at Rio Janeiro and Teneriffe on the homeward voyage.

Shaw, Saville, and Albion Company. Monthly steamers *viâ* Cape of Good Hope, calling also at Rio and Teneriffe on the homeward voyage.

NEW ZEALAND TO SYDNEY AND MELBOURNE.

The Union Steam Shipping Company run one of their fine steamers weekly from one or other of the New Zealand ports to Sydney and Melbourne.

The San Francisco Mail steamers also run from Auckland to Sydney.

TO AUSTRALIAN PORTS.

Peninsular and Oriental Company, *viâ* Suez Canal.

Orient Steam Company, *viâ* Suez Canal.

Messageries Maritimes, from Marseilles, *viâ* Suez Canal.

Nord Deutscher Lloyd's, from Antwerp, *viâ* Suez Canal.

Eastern and Australasian Steam Shipping Company, from Hong Kong to Brisbane, calling at Thursday Island.

Queensland Royal Mail Company, London to Brisbane, *viâ* Suez Canal, calling at Java.

TO NEW GUINEA.

A steamer has lately been put on from Thursday Island.

The New Guinea Company of Berlin also intends running a steamer in connection with the Nord Deutscher Lloyd's.

To Fiji.

Union Steam Shipping Company, monthly from Auckland.

Australasian United Steam Navigation Company, monthly from Sydney.

To New Caledonia.

Australasian United Steam Navigation Company monthly to Noumea, from Sydney.

To Samoa and Tonga.

Steamer *Lubeck* connecting with Nord Deutscher Lloyd's from Sydney.

To Tahiti.

Donald and Edenborough, monthly from Auckland, calling at Rarotonga and intermediate islands.

It is not necessary to mention the splendid steamers belonging to the various companies and firms which keep up communication along the New Zealand and Australian coasts; nor the railway system becoming so rapidly developed as to render communication between all the great centres constant and daily, both in Australia and New Zealand. It is sufficient to say that the facilities for travel and intercommunication are constantly improving, and population and commerce rapidly increasing.

www.ingramcontent.com/pod-product-compliance
Lightning Source LLC
Chambersburg PA
CBHW020236240426
43672CB00006B/550